Quilts
SOLD!

Quilts SOLD!

A guide to heirloom and antique quilts

BY DAVE & KATHY PROCHNOW

PELICAN PUBLISHING COMPANY

Gretna 2006

*The word "Pelican" and the depiction of a pelican are trademarks
of Pelican Publishing Company, Inc., and are registered in the
U.S. Patent and Trademark Office.*

Library of Congress Cataloging-in-Publication Data

Prochnow, Dave.
  Quilts sold! : a guide to heirloom and antique quilts / by Dave and Kathy Prochnow.
     p. cm.
  Includes index.
  ISBN-13: 978-1-58980-375-6 (hardcover : alk. paper)
  1. Quilts—Collectors and collecting—United States. 2. Quilts—Prices. 3. Quilts—Patterns. I.
Prochnow, Kathy. II. Title.
  NK9112.P76 2006
  746.46075—dc22

                       2005033058

Printed in China

Published by Pelican Publishing Company, Inc.
1000 Burmaster Street, Gretna, Louisiana 70053

Contents

Preface

Experiencing a thrill similar to that of finding a remarkable quilt tucked away in the corner of an estate sale, I am extremely pleased to showcase the outstanding talent of Kathy Prochnow in the pages of this book. Kathy is a gifted quilter who continually strives to achieve perfection in her dedicated, loving attention for reproducing landmark antique quilts. It is this same "pioneer" spirit that Kathy has ably demonstrated in her quilting that has guided my attempt at bringing the collecting of antique quilts back to life through this massive compilation of auction house sale results. This is an effort that spans over fifteen years of meticulous record keeping, which resulted in a library's worth of catalogs, auction announcements, and quilt sale descriptions.

In addition to Kathy's untiring tutelage during my fledging quilting years, I also received outstanding contributions from Butterfield's, Christie's, Cowan's Auctions, James Julia, Ken Farmer Auctions & Appraisals, Pook & Pook, Skinner, Sloan's, and Thomaston Place Auction Galleries auction houses. Much of the beautiful photography in this book is due to the relentless research of the public relations and marketing departments from these auction houses. In particular, I would like to thank Katherine Adler, William Gage, Jill Z. McBride, D. Levi Morgan, Kellie Seltzer, Kelly Taylor, Anne Trodella, Kaja Veilleux, and Dawn Wilbur.

There are also numerous manufacturers that I would like to acknowledge who supported the development of this book. These invaluable contributors include April Atchley, Susan Bogard, Jodi Bushman, Jill Clarvit, Pat DeSantis, Carla Horvath, Patricia Lee, Daena Oczachowski, Vickie Paullus, Robert Purcell, Kathy Rickel, Vicki Smith, Andreea Sparhawk, Jacque Tupper, and Tracy Whitlock.

—Dave Prochnow
26 May 2005

Acknowledgments

The following products, manufacturers, and auction houses generously contributed to the development of this book:

Archivart®

Christie's

Cowan's Auctions, Inc.

Debbie Mumm, Inc.

Fairfield

Fiskars

Gingher, Inc.

James D. Julia, Inc.

Janome

Ken Farmer Auctions & Appraisals LLC

Kyle Sanchez, RJR Fabrics

Marcus Brothers Textiles, Inc.

Mountain Mist, Stearns Technical Textiles Co.

Pauma R. Deaton, communications manager, Prym-Dritz

Pook & Pook, Inc.

Robison-Anton Textiles

Skinner, Inc.

Sloan's

Sulky Products

Superior Threads, Inc.

Thomaston Place Auction Galleries

The Warm Company

Wrights

YLI Corporation

Although estimated at $500 to $1,000, this remarkable coxcomb and rose quilt, circa 1860-1880, was sold by Cowan's Auctions for $1,610 in 2004. (Photograph courtesy of Cowan's Auctions, Inc.)

Buying History

A Short Lesson in Creating Quilt Reproductions from Auction House Originals

Antique quilts are big business. Nowhere is this proclamation more readily apparent than at the major auction houses of the United States. From New York City to San Francisco, America's auctioneers are selling antique quilts at a fever pitch. Similarly, investors are lining up to pay top dollars for these historically significant quilts. More and more frequently, these prices rival the bids that have been traditionally reserved for high-profile fine-art pieces. This ability to attract the attention of serious buyers signals the ascent of the antique quilt to the status of important Americana.

The six major auction houses in the United States that regularly sell antique quilts are:
- Butterfields
- Christie's
- James D. Julia
- Skinner
- Sloan's
- Sotheby's

Butterfields

Butterfields was the first major auction house to embrace the Internet. By publishing its sales catalogs online and conducting "live" sales via eBay, Butterfields continues to demonstrate the same pioneering sprit that was essential for their establishment in San Francisco, California, during the western United States' 1865 gold rush. As it continued to prosper in the vast West Coast antique market, Butterfields opened a second gallery in Los Angeles in 1988 and merged with Dunning's of Illinois in 1998. Furthermore, Butterfields helped to put a human face on the

A Log Cabin quilt, a pair of Bethlehem Star pillow cases, and a jacquard wool coverlet that Christie's sold for $345, $1,725, and $575, respectively, during an auction in 1999. (Photograph courtesy of Christie's Images Ltd. 1999)

11

This Bethlehem Star quilt was sold by Sloan's in 1996 for $3,000. (Photograph courtesy of Sloan's)

stodgy appearance of antique collecting by casting its expert appraisers on numerous educational and cable television programs.

Since the early days of antique quilt trading, Butterfields has been known as a leading source for fine and rare Amish quilts. This early foothold in quilt sales has enabled Butterfields to expand its listings to include some great sales of late-nineteenth-century appliqué quilts and crazy quilts in 2001 and 2002.

Christie's

Christie's is the world's oldest auction house for fine-art objects. The beginning of Christie's distinguished history in auctioning began in London, England, on December 5, 1766.

From this date forward, Christie's has been the site of many important events in the sale of European art. For example, Catherine the Great of Russia purchased the collection of Sir Robert Walpole through Christie's for installation in the Hermitage. Similarly, the collections of Sir Joshua Reynolds and the Duke of Buckingham were auctioned at Christie's throughout the 1700s and 1800s.

It wasn't until 1977–1979, however, when Christie's opened its two landmark New York City auction houses, that the firm became world renowned for its sales in art works other than paintings: books, furniture, jewelry, porcelain, wine, automobiles, and quilts. In these new domestic auction houses, Christie's offered the collections of Henry Ford II, Paul Mellon, and Billy Wilder. This exposure enabled buyers and sellers to realize that premium prices could be obtained from the sale of art objects similar to those that had been reserved for van Gogh paintings.

James D. Julia

This Fairfield, Maine, auction house was founded in the mid-1960s by Arthur Julia. Purchased by Arthur's son, James D. Julia, in 1974, the firm specializes in firearms, toys and dolls, and American antiques. Building on this firearm specialization, James D. Julia successfully brokered one of the most expensive American firearms sales in April 2000, when a Winchester Model 66 attributed to the Battle of the Little Big Horn sold for $684,500. Although firearms have received the higher profile sales from this Northeast auction house, various American ephemera, including some beautiful quilts, have been sold at auction by James D. Julia.

Skinner, Inc.

Known for fielding a crew of expert appraisers on the popular PBS-TV show *Antiques Roadshow*, this Massachusetts full-service auctioneer regularly conducts year-round sales of antique quilts. Though typically a part of massive American furniture and decorative arts sales, quilt sales at Skinner occasionally will be assembled into unlikely categories. For example, a recent sale contained two lots of over twenty antique doll quilts in a special holiday toys, dolls, and collectibles show. In terms of record-setting quilt prices, Skinner held the record in 2002 when they auctioned the legendary "Scenes of Childhood" appliquéd quilt for a remarkable $30,550. (See Chapter 8 for more information about this remarkable quilt.)

Sloan's

Sloan's was founded in 1853 by Latimer and Cleary. In 1891, C. G. Sloan purchased the Latimer and Cleary gallery and renamed the auction house after himself. The auction gallery was originally located at Eleventh Street and Pennsylvania Avenue in Washington, D.C. Throughout its history, Sloan's has remained in Washington, D.C; in January 1997, however, they opened another auction house in Miami, Florida. Today, Sloan's features at least one sale per year spotlighting antique quilts.

Sotheby's

Founded in 1744 as an auctioneer of property, manors, and

Some collectors specialize in buying specific quilt patterns such as this crazy quilt.

estates, Sotheby's has a rich heritage of assembling exciting collections of memorabilia into huge sales. These sales can actually take on a life of their own and become almost as entertaining as the items themselves.

Sotheby's established itself in the United States by acquiring the Parke Bernet auction house in 1964. For thirty-two years, the Parke Bernet house (founded by Maj. Hiram Parke and Otto Bernet) reigned as the leading gallery, catering to the growing population of financial elite in America. Originally named Sotheby Parke Bernet, Sotheby's has become a viable competitor to Christie's in the sale of fine-art objects in the United States.

It was Sotheby's, though, that initiated the sales of collectible indigenous art objects. Quilts, weathervanes, and duck decoys soon became the sales staple of the Sotheby Parke Bernet auction house. Remarkably, in 1979 the sale of the Gregory collection enabled folk-art prices to break the one-million-dollar mark. Today, while the name of the Sotheby Parke Bernet house has been simplified to Sotheby's, the legacy of folk-art sales continues with yearly sales of outstanding quilt collections.

Knowing the major players in today's estate sale scene is only half the contest; you must also know how to play the game. As such, two of the foremost factors that contribute to the awarding of a successful bid are learning to accurately judge the condition of an antique quilt and preparing yourself with a credible history of past and present quilt valuations at auction.

While Chapter 1 provides you with an excellent overview of learning how to read antique quilts, one of the most comprehensive listings of actual prices realized at auctions over the past ten years has been packed into Chapter 5. In order to make this massive listing a manageable reference, the prices have been cataloged according to major American quilt types and patterns. Therefore, before you submit a bid for a rare African American Robbing Peter to Pay Paul quilt, thumb through Chapter 5 and study the pricing history for this particular pattern. Likewise, don't forget to bone up on learning how to read quilt history in Chapter 1. Your ability to garner winning quilt bids could be a direct reflection of your mastering of these two chapters.

Making Your Own Auction House Original

Understanding the auction value of a quilt as well as where to find these pieces of Americana is important for collectors, but you can also bring the beauty and tradition of antique quilts into the home through reproductions. There are three simple steps that you should follow for making an accurate reproduction of any antique quilt that is sold at auction.

Research. Locate a suitable quilt. The best method for finding a good quilt candidate is from the sales catalogs that are published by each auction house. In Appendix A, you can obtain addresses for all of the major auction houses. Chapter 3 provides you with all of the ammunition that you will need for successfully placing a winning bid.

Quilt reproductions can be cozy additions for any home.

Pattern. Design your pattern. There are a variety of techniques that you can use for making an accurate pattern from a photograph printed in an auction house catalog. There are four unique quilt patterns provided for you in Chapter 8. All of the steps needed for turning a photograph into a quilt pattern are described in Chapter 7.

Quilt. Assemble your quilt. After you have created a pattern from the original quilt, turn your inspiration into a perfect reproduction. If you'd like some pointers for sharpening your quilting skills, Chapter 6 contains valuable information on mastering both handmade as well as machine-made quilting. Furthermore, accurate reproduction fabrics are currently being offered by various manufacturers. In Chapter 2, a complete

Seamlessly blending heirloom quilts into traditional home décor is rapidly becoming a popular interior design motif for the new millennium.

listing of historically accurate fabrics will help you find that perfect match for making your reproduction the spitting image of the original.

As a sample demonstration, let's apply these three simple steps to an outstanding quilt that was sold at a Christie's auction in late 1998.

Research

While most of today's significant antique quilts are sold in American auction houses, there is a growing interest in the sale of the textile arts throughout Europe. In fact, Christie's in Zurich, Switzerland, offered a beautiful American quilt in their third house sale of 1998.

Not all auctions are held at Christie's main offices, however. In rare cases, the breadth of the collection warrants that the sale be held on the grounds of the seller's home. These events are occasionally called house sales. In 1998, several of these house sales were sponsored by Christie's European salesrooms. The first two house sales were held in England and Germany. While antique quilts weren't commonplace at either of these first two sales, the third event contained an enormous selection of fabulous textile arts.

Backed by the successes of the Hackwood Park sale in England and the collections of Princess Reuss in Germany, Christie's auctioned off the contents of the Herblingen Castle during a five-day sale in Switzerland. Officially dubbed Schloss Herblingen-Schaffhausen, this mid-September 1998 sale featured the collected works of antique dealers Hindrik Nieboer and Max Rutishauser. Amid exquisite furniture, porcelain, and silver there were two hundred lots of quilts and other assorted textiles.

The diversity of dates found in this remarkable collection of textiles served as a "crash course" on the history of European decorative arts. Ranging from cushion covers and wall hangings to quilts and tapestries, this sale was an impressive reminder of the financial worth that a well-made quilt can attract.

The oldest quilt member of this sale was a Genevese example dated to 1884. In contrast to this modest 119-year-old quilt, there was a sixteenth-century German embroidered wool tapestry depicting three angels visiting Abraham and Sarah, which captured one of the higher textile bids.

Pattern

Aside from these splendid continental offerings there was one American quilt that demonstrated the mastery of quilting that Yankee women had achieved over their motherland. Plainly labeled as "Quilt, Amerikanisch," this handsomely appliquéd quilt unfortunately held an equally plain provenance.

Unlike many collections, the Herblingen Castle lots were sprinkled throughout the property and used in functioning dining areas, studies, and bedrooms. In fact, this American quilt was used as the principle bed covering inside a very blue bedroom.

Dated at early twentieth century, this 82-inch by 84-inch joined quilt contained four light gold cornflowers outlined in red and interlaced with four dark blue leaves. The field for the cornflowers was ecru and heavily quilted. Framing the border of this quilt was a draped red sash symbolically held with a series of knotted dark blue and red tassels.

As a footnote, the actual bidding for this quilt was remarkably

While the quilt reproductions in this book should not be considered exact replicas, they can bring a close approximation of authentic Americana into any quilt collection.

strong. The pre-auction estimate ranged from $790 to $1,300. During the auction, however, the final winning bid was $1,169.28. The odd dollar amount is attributed to the exchange rate from Swiss francs to US dollars.

Quilt

Now that the acquisition and designing legwork has been completed, the reproduction is ready to take form.

Step 1. To make one block from this quilt, establish a list of fabrics.

Fabric Requirements:
1 yard ecru
1 yard red
¼ yard light yellow
¼ yard dark blue

Step 2. Determine how many pieces of fabric are needed and cut out the pattern. For this block, you can use a raw-edge appliqué technique for assembling on a sewing machine. Therefore, you can cut out the exact shape of each pattern.

Step 3. Mark the background fabric for placement of the pattern.

Step 4. Position the yellow strips onto the blue petals, choose the appliqué quilting stitch on your sewing machine, and stitch around the gold fabric strips.

Step 5. Repeat Step 4 using the yellow petals and the red petals.

Step 6. Repeat the process with the yellow star and the red star.

Step 7. Using your sewing machine stitch around each of the petals and attach them to the background fabric.

Step 8. Position the star in the middle of the block, making sure that the ends of the petals are covered; stitch around the star.

There you have it, an accurate reproduction block of an antique quilt sold at a major auction house in 1998. In the following pages, you will learn to appreciate the value that can be derived from collecting antique quilts, as well as discover many more quilt projects that will enable you to assemble an outstanding collection of auction block quilts.

Handsome reproductions of heirloom quilts that have been sold at auction can be made with modern fabrics and machine sewing.

Whether your technique is traditional hand quilting or modern sewing-machine quilting, quilt reproductions can be a cost-effective way of supplementing your antique quilt collection.

The subject for our first attempt at making a quilt reproduction was this appliquéd quilt, which was auctioned by Christie's Zurich in 1998. The winning bid for this quilt was $1,169.28. (Photograph courtesy of Christie's)

Most quilts sold at auction were formerly functional household elements. As in this case, the suitably named "Blue Bedroom" of Schloss Herblingen (Herblingen Castle) in Switzerland makes good use of this appliquéd quilt. (Photograph courtesy of Christie's)

Drawing of a Baltimore Album quilt dated March 4, 1841.

1

Reading an Antique Quilt

How old is it? This simple question is the bane of every quilt collector who attends an auction in the hopes of walking away with a treasure. There is, however, no simple formula that can be used for determining the age of a quilt. For example, we had an adventure in provenance at a notable quilt auction.

During the 1995 auction of the Dr. and Mrs. Henry P. Deyerle collection in Charlottesville, Virginia, Sotheby's sold two beautiful quilts from the mid-nineteenth century. Each quilt was expected to fetch bids somewhere in the ballpark of $2,000 to $15,000.

The Deyerles were avid collectors of American antiques. Educated as a surgeon, Dr. Deyerle became his own "curator" of a priceless assembly of vintage furniture, period porcelain, and classic American paintings. Being skilled in scientific research, Dr. Deyerle was extremely adept at recording every conceivable historical element of each artifact in his collection. This meticulous attention to detail is one of the distinctive features that made this auction a prominent showcase for priceless antiques.

All told there were five different quilts in the Deyerle collection. In order to facilitate a more active bidding process, each of these quilts was cataloged as a separate lot during the two-day auction, a frequent practice by auction houses with items that possess a high reserve. According to the historical research assembled by the quilts' previous owners, these quilts all dated from the nineteenth century. Although only one quilt, a Baltimore Album, was dated, an estimated historical record for the remaining lots was determined through fiber and cloth analysis. This scientific validation, plus the provenance associated with two of the other lots, made the quilts in the Deyerle collection especially noteworthy.

The first quilt was a brightly colored piece measuring 100 inches by 100 inches. Nine red, green, white, and blue cotton-blossom and bud appliqués were beautifully quilted over a brilliant orange cotton field. A pineapple and feather wreath quilting was used throughout this field inside the sawtooth border. Although not officially dated, this quilt bore a provenance stating a prior sale from the Dr. Stuart estate in Winchester, Virginia. It sold for $2,070.

In this same collection, an exquisite Baltimore Album quilt was also featured. Bearing a March 4, 1841, date, the 96-inch by 97-inch quilt combined red, green, yellow, and blue calico with various solid fabrics into twenty-five blocks. The center of this Baltimore Album was highlighted by a spread-winged American eagle-with-flag block, and a delicate feather-and-diagonal-line quilting was applied throughout the quilt. In witness of the quilt's heritage, several of its squares were both signed and dated. This incredible demonstration of quilting mastery was sold for $5,462.

In "reading" these quilts, we were able to determine a valid age through the abundance of historical information that had been assembled by the collection's owners. But what if we weren't so lucky? How could we have assured ourselves that these were vintage quilts?

There are five techniques that can and cannot be accurately used for assessing a quilt's approximate age.

Pattern. This is a false indicator of age. Many of today's contemporary geometric designs, for example, can trace their roots to some of the earliest quilt makers. In her helpful article, "A Chronological Index to Pieced Quilt Patterns: 1775-1825,"[1] Barbara Brackman attempts to promote a classification scheme for indexing and, hopefully, dating quilts based on the chronological appearance of a given quilt pattern. While the volume of work depicted in this article is impressive, its value towards dating quilts

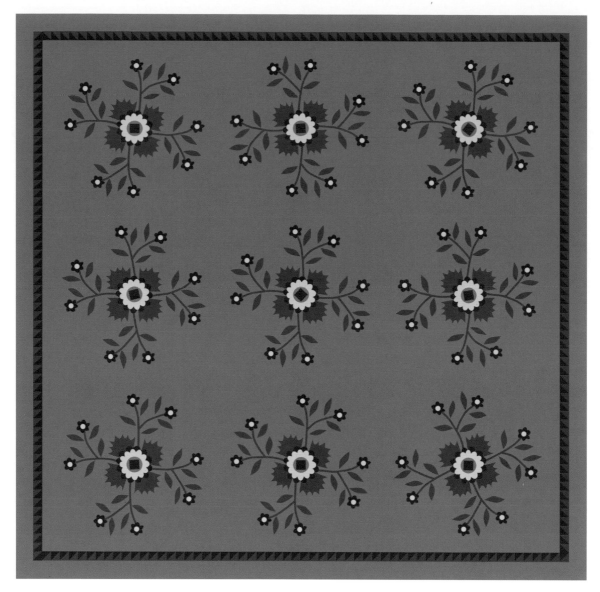

*Drawing of a pieced and appliquéd cotton quilt, Pennsylvania,
mid-nineteenth century.*

is questionable. Even Ms. Brackman states, "The majority of the early patterns are still in use."[2] She later indicates that "the quilts made in these designs today look essentially like their earlier counterparts."[3]

Technique. This can be a dubious method for determining age. Many beginning quilt collectors incorrectly believe that the presence of cotton seeds in a batting is a sign of vintage origin. Since most quilts were a labor of love, women spent many hours combing the distasteful seeds from their batting. Conversely, many quilt forgers are using cotton seeds today as a false indicator of age. Quilt expert Stella Rubin takes this cause

two steps further by claiming that the purported seeds are more likely plant fragments and more importantly, that these impurities can be found in "quilts that were made well into the 20th century."[4]

Bindings. Braiding, bias folds, homespun tape, and hemstitching are common vintage methods of binding the edges of a quilt. Although most quilters duplicate the technique of their grandmothers, a careful study of a quilt's binding can be an indication of age. Another clue for determining the age of a quilt's binding is through the usage of bias-cut fabric. According to Roderick Kiracofe, you can generally attribute

Amish Quilt Aging

Homespun and home-dyed fabrics; dark earth tone colors; complex feather patterns	Early nineteenth century
Homespun and home-dyed fabrics; lighter colors; more complex patterns; dense stitching count	1870-1890
Commercial fabric; home-dyed vibrant colors; more geometric patterns	1890-1920
Commercial fabric; blue color tones; white backgrounds	1920-1930
Poor fabric quality; lighter colors; reduced stitch density	1930-1940
Synthetic fabrics; pastel colors; reduced stitch density; simple patterns	1940-1950
Polyester fabrics; stronger colors; simple patterns	1950-1960
Commercial fabrics; machine stitching	1960-Present

straight-grain binding fabrics to nineteenth-century quilts, while the twentieth-century (and, certainly, the twenty-first century) quilts typically opted for a bias-cut binding.[5] Unfortunately, the counterfeiters are one step ahead of the collectors; a straight-grain binding can be hand sewn over the row of machine stitching that fixes the binding to the quilt's edge.[6] Only careful examination of this type of quilt will prevent you from investing a king's ransom in a fool's game.

> You can quickly judge the "approximate" age of an antique quilt by examining its binding. Simply flatten out the binding with your fingers and study the wear along the edge or crease of the binding. A well-worn binding edge signals an older quilt.

Appliqué. The use of distinct visual imagery can be a great source of historical information. Eagles, flags, famous figures, and even unique fabric colors can be used for estimating a quilt's age. For example, the 1929 Lone Eagle quilt by Emma Tyrrell contains top view appliqués of Charles Lindbergh's Ryan NYP *Spirit of St. Louis* aircraft, which he used for flying solo across the Atlantic Ocean on May 20-21, 1927. This appliqué is a terrific example of a dateable attribute since the Ryan NYP was first flown in 1927. The widespread publication of Ms. Tyrrell's pattern, however, allowed Lone Eagle copies to be made well into the early 1930s.

Textiles. Restricted to the domain of the scientist or expert conservationist, studying the chemical composition of textile fibers and dyes can be the best method for exacting a reasonably accurate age for a quilt. Luckily, a great deal of published research literature is available for attempting to date fabrics and dyes. Without a doubt, one of the most frequently misunderstood dyes is the so-called Turkey Red. Generally credited to a random lot of fabric dyers from the region around the Mediterranean Sea, the production of colorfast red dye from Rubiaceae plants (e.g., madder) containing alizarin was commercially available from 1600-1930.[7] Unfortunately, unscrupulous vendors would often palm off their Congo Reds (ca. 1860-1900) and vat reds (ca. 1910-1920) as Turkey Red, but each of the other red dyes had a varying degree of fastness, brilliance, and color saturation that was clearly differentiable from the alizarin reds.[8] You can even occasionally see this misused appellation practice in discount fabric stores today.

An even better tool for reliably determining a quilt's age is education. The best education comes from research and library study combined with a trip to one or more auction houses. In a quilt sale at Sotheby's, this latter approach was useful for judging the worth of several Baltimore Album quilts.

According to Roderick Kiracofe in his definitive tome on America's textile history, *The American Quilt,* the lineage of the Baltimore Album quilt can be directly traced to the work of two women: Achsah Goodwin Wilkins and Mary Evans.[9] Both the elder Wilkins and her protégé Evans belonged to a group called the "Ladies of Baltimore." Under the expert guidance of Mrs. Wilkins, gifted quilt makers like Mary Evans performed the needlework for creating this unique appliquéd work.

There are some quilt historians, however, who claim Mary Evans was a nom de plume for any sewing member of the "Ladies of Baltimore." This theory is supported by Eleanor Hamilton Sienkiewicz, who concludes that it would have been difficult for a single woman to have created all of the Baltimore Album quilts that bear the mark "Mary Evans." In fact, Sienkiewicz has speculated that the real Mary Evans would have had to devote a year's worth of forty-hour weeks to the creation of a single Baltimore Album quilt. Therefore, it is doubtful that a single individual is responsible for all the quilts inscribed with her name.

Prices, as well as the collector's demand, increase when a quilt can be document-ed with the quilter's name and its creation date. Sloan's auctioned this Dora Ann Cox quilt, circa 1840, for $5,000 in 1999. (Photograph courtesy of Sloan's)

In early October, 1998, Sotheby's held an auction of fine Americana that featured two outstanding examples of Baltimore Album quilts. Likewise, the estimated bid prices for these fine pieces reflected the type of devotion that Ms. Sienkiewicz had speculated was required for creating this type of quilt.

The first of these two lots was a mid-nineteenth-century example that bore the signatures of Mary Foster and Elizabeth Holland. This 99-inch by 99-inch Baltimore-style album quilt consisted of twenty-five squares, each bordered with a dark red edge. Each square contained red, green, yellow, beige, and blue fabrics. The hallmark of this quilt, however, was the center square. In the center of the quilt there was the spread-winged American eagle motif, which is commonplace among the Baltimore Album quilts. The eagle's beak held an olive branch, while its claws grasped a vine along with the American flag. Finally, the quilting throughout the white cotton field was exquisite. Echo, clamshell, and diamond stitching lent consider-able depth to this outstanding quilt.

Sotheby's had placed an estimated sale price of between $12,000 and $18,000 for this Baltimore Album quilt. During the actual auction, the quilt commanded a winning bid of $8,625.

Modern quilting products like Sulky stabilizers are ideal for creating your own quilt reproductions.

On a slightly smaller scale, another Baltimore Album estimated at $8,000 to $12,000 fetched $8,050. This quilt, dated circa 1860, measured 60 inches by 60 inches. Like its more lavish auction-mate, this example used red, green, yellow, and blue fabrics to form twenty-five non-bordered blocks. Similarly, the center square featured an eagle grasping floral vines and perched on a bunting-clad branch.

While either of these Baltimore Album quilts would have made Achsah Goodwin Wilkins proud of her legacy, another album-like quilt stole the show during this October auction. A crewel-embroidered quilt by Angeline Nowlen that was dated May 23, 1864, displayed outstanding diamond, leaf, flower, and sunburst quilting patterns. Furthermore, an elegant embroidered vine and flower border framed the forty-two blocks of this 68-inch by 78-inch masterpiece. Exceeding the bids for the more traditional Baltimore Albums, the winning bid for this quilt was $9,200.

During your quilt dating experiences, remember to keep this practice at the top of your age-determining techniques: always date for time spans and not for years. In other words, make your date determination in twenty-five to fifty-year time spans rather than attempting to narrow the field of choices to a specific year. Not only will you be rewarded with a satisfying completion to your quilt research work, you will also avoid the embarrassment of an incorrect guess!

This reproduction of a Skinner-auctioned quilt adds the perfect splash of patriotic color to a modern living room during special-occasion national holidays.

The chaotic nature of the crazy quilt appeals to a wide range of collectors, making this pattern extremely collectable.

The variations in the blue fabric used in this Irish Chain pattern that was sold by Christie's in 1999 for $1,150 make this quilt a visual treat to view. (Photograph courtesy of Christie's Images Ltd 1999)

Delicate fabrics like the material used in this crazy quilt should be professionally examined by a trained textile archivist.

2

Getting the Goods on Antique Fabrics

If quilting is the soul of a quilt, then fabric must be its flesh. Yet fabric was cherished by early quilt makers and held with a respect that rivaled a religious zeal. Spinning, weaving, and dyeing were the daily activities required for producing yards of usable fabric for both clothing and quilts. Prior to the development of commercial fabrics, the production of fabric was undertaken by women in their homes. Throughout the late eighteenth century and early nineteenth century, numerous advances in the production of cotton, yarn, and dye helped streamline this home-grown process of making fabric. It wasn't until 1814 and the advent of the power loom in America that commercial fabrics became a viable alternative to home spinning and weaving. In fact, at the start of the American Civil War commercial fabric production had replaced home manufacture as the leading source of usable fabric.

A Short History of Making Patterned Fabric

As early as 1749, patterns were being applied to fabrics in a commercial setting. These efforts were laborious and required a great deal of precision in the application of the pattern. Slowly mechanical conveniences shortened the production cycle and reduced the dependency on highly skilled craftsmen. There are three generally accepted historical methods for applying patterns to fabric.

Block Printing. This technique is the most labor-intensive method of applying a pattern to fabric. Typically, a wooden block would be charged with a selected dye and then pressed against the fabric. Each pressing of the wooden block would have to be registered against the previous application. This registration technique enabled fabric designers to combine similar blocks charged with various colors of dye into spectacular multi-colored patterns.

You can still find heirloom quilt treasures at reasonable prices. In 2002, James Julia auctioned this 1847 friendship quilt for $316.25! (Photograph courtesy of James D. Julia, Inc.)

These ingenious block makers used metal strips, wire, and felt to alter the application of the dye. For example, metal strips were used as outlines and precise shapes in the creation of braidlike patterns. Similarly, wire was hammered into the wooden block for making picotage designs. Finally, felt was attached to the blocks for helping flood large areas of fabric with solid color.

The life span of block printing came to an end in the mid-1800s. However, it has enjoyed a revival throughout the latter half of the nineteenth century and early twentieth century.

Copperplate Printing. Based on the intaglio printing process used in the paper industry, copperplate printing shared several similarities with block printing. Known as plates, each block of copperplate printing, like block printing, was applied in registered patterns. Likewise, dye was applied to each plate prior to pressing against the fabric. Unlike block printing, however, copperplate printing relied on the design being either acid etched or hand engraved into the plates, rather than applied to its surface.

There was one distinctive attribute of copperplate printing

that distinguished it from block printing: copperplate patterns were usually solid monochrome colors. Largely done in reds, blues, and blacks, elaborate scenes were applied to fabrics as toiles. These toiles are sometimes called toiles of Jouy. Jouy was the home of the well-known French fabric firm Oberkampf. During the late eighteenth century, Oberkampf reigned as the most prolific manufacturer of patterned fabrics in the world. Copperplate printing was popular during the same period as block printing, with 1830 signaling the demise of this fanciful patterning technique.

Roller Printing. The birth of modern fabric pattern application can be traced to 1785, the year Thomas Bell obtained his patent for a water-powered roller printing process. Although Oberkampf claims to have invented the roller process prior to Bell, historians generally credit the Scotsman with its invention. Like the slightly automated copperplate printing processes, roller printing relied on engraved plates for applying the pattern to the fabric; however, this is where all similarity between the two methods ends.

Roller printing used copper cylinders for holding the pattern. These cylinders were either acid etched or hand engraved with the fabric's design. Dye was held in a tray that bathed the rotating cylinder, and long, continuous lengths of fabric were then fed between the dye-charged cylinder and its closely associated backing drum.

With the invention of roller printing, printed fabrics were available to both European and American quilters at a reasonable price. Whereas a block-applied pattern would take twelve to fifteen hours of skilled labor, a similar roller-printed fabric would be ready in under two minutes. The result of this mechanical advance was the mass production of patterned fabrics. So pervasive was the use of roller-printed fabrics that after 1830 quilts featuring patterned fabrics were commonly made by the roller printing process.

Modern Fabric Reproductions

One of the problems with attempting to create a reproduction of a historic quilt is simulating the look and feel of block, copperplate, and roller-printed fabrics. There are only three manufacturers who specialize in the reproduction of historic fabrics, but Benartex, Debbie Mumm, Marcus Brothers Textiles, P&B Textiles, and RJR Fashion Fabrics offer a wide assortment of patterned fabrics that can be matched to many of the quilts that are currently being sold at auction houses.

If you are going to make a quilt reproduction, choose your fabric palette carefully. Many of our modern fabrics are inappropriate for simulating an heirloom quilt.

There are many textile manufacturers that specialize in historic fabric reproductions, which lend themselves to historic quilt patterns.

These manufacturers typically rely on the extensive fabric collections housed at the National Society Daughters of the American Revolution (DAR) Museum and the Shelburne Museum. Based on these historical collections, each manufacturer has assembled fabric patterns into reproduction and adaptation catalogs.

Caring for Historical Fabrics

Whether you've purchased an antique quilt or created your own reproduction from an auction house catalog, you should actively preserve your treasure before it fades from your collection and is retained only in your memories. Regardless of the origin of your acquisition, like any work of art, a quilt must be properly cleaned and stored.

Whatever the cleaning technique, be careful not to damage the fabric beyond the normal wear and tear that accumulates on a quilt through normal use—this type of intrusive restoration can lessen the value of the quilt and might even lead to a serious compromise of the quilt's integrity. Similarly, be wary of attempting even the simplest cleaning process without a high degree of expertise in fabric conservation. Once you understand all the precautions associated with fabric restoration and care, there are a couple of simple cleaning tasks that you can consider for minimizing the effects of common quilt ailments. For example, steam can be used for breathing new life into flattened batting. This process is wrought with precautions, however, ranging from the scorching of fabric to the deleterious soaking of the batting.[1]

One of the least appreciated means (by today's quilt collector) of cleaning a quilt is also one of the most time-honored methods: airing. Lay the quilt outdoors on a flat, sheltered surface that has been protected with an appropriately sized cotton sheet and make sure the quilt is protected from direct sunlight.[2] Several good airings can work wonders at "breathing new life" into an antique quilt.

The four most destructive agents to a quilt are dirt, light, moisture, and acid. Proper handling and storage procedures can greatly reduce the potential damage caused by these four agents.

Dirt. The accumulation of dirt can be as common as the settling of dust on a quilt covering a bed. This dust can actually stain a quilt's fabric as humidity and temperature conditions change in the house. Once either dust or dirt becomes moist and stains the fabric, restoration must be performed by a trained fabric conservationist.

If your quilt becomes covered with a light coating of dry dirt or dust, you can clean it with a vacuum cleaner and a sheet of fiberglass window screen. Simply lay the window screen over the quilt's surface, being careful not to snag the fabric. Set the vacuum cleaner to a low-power setting and slowly move its nozzle over the window screen's surface. Hold the nozzle approximately one to two inches above the surface of the quilt. This technique will remove any dry dirt and dust from the surface of the fabric without distorting the quilt or damaging its batting.

Light. All fabrics will age and usually discolor when exposed to ultraviolet sunlight. Even commercial fluorescent lighting can accelerate this aging process. While these factors

Displaying your quilt collection inside your home is a growing interior design trend.

can present a serious limitation on the display of quilts for public appreciation, there are three simple precautions that you can take to ensure that light will not damage your quilt.

1. Avoid all direct exposure of the fabric to sunlight.
2. Reduce the intensity of all room lighting to a subdued level.
3. Make sure that spotlights and other bright lights do not shine directly on the fabric's surface.

If some of these precautions are impossible to control, you can mount your quilt behind a panel of ultraviolet-filtering glazing (e.g., Light Impressions archival catalog; 800-828-6216, www.lightimpressionsdirect.com). This technique has been used by museums for displaying photographs in public settings.

Budding quilt collectors should learn the basics of archival textile preservation prior to investing in auction house sales. Storage products like Archivart are well-suited for holding heirloom quilts.

Many professional and lay quilt conservationists have stated that flash photography contributes to the deterioration of quilt fabrics. However, there are two factors to consider before you seclude your quilt collection in a lightless vault. First, the duration of a standard commercial professional flash unit lasts shorter than one thousandth of a second. This exposure is insufficient for accelerating the fabric's aging process. Furthermore, a professional flash photography system consists of reflective umbrellas that can absorb many of the light's more damaging UV properties. Secondly, if fabric deterioration from ultraviolet exposure is an issue with your antique quilt collection, inexpensive UV filters can be purchased for most professional electronic flash units. These filters screen the harmful UV rays from the light without adversely affecting the photograph's color. If you have additional questions about flash photography, please consult with a professional photographer.

Moisture. Some older fabrics utilized dyes that were soluble in water. Therefore, moisture, condensation, and humidity can cause these dyes to run and stain other portions of a quilt. Historically, water was used in the cleaning of fabrics, but these water cleaning techniques could deposit salts on the fabric that would discolor quilts. Only a trained textile conservationist should attempt to clean moisture stains from antique quilt fabrics.

Acid. Even the most well-intentioned quilt storage techniques can cause severe damage to historical fabrics. Plastics, certain fiber materials, and ordinary paper products can release acids that will stain or degrade quilt fabrics. The best remedy for reducing the possibility of acid contamination is through buffered or acid-free paper and muslin.

In practice, the reduction of acid contamination to a quilt requires that you have a large acid-free storage container along with several sheets of buffered paper or muslin. Line the container with the muslin and gently lay the quilt in the box. If the quilt is larger than the container, the quilt must be folded or rolled. As you fold or roll the quilt, interleave a sheet of buffered paper between each layer of fabric. Make sure that you do not crease the quilt along each fold or place another quilt on top of the folded quilt. You should periodically unfold (or unroll) the quilt and check it for damage. Afterwards, refold the quilt in a different fold sequence.

Archivart® is the leading supplier of textile conservation products. They specialize in acid-free and buffered papers and storage boxes. Museums and libraries use their products for the preservation of paper and canvas art. In addition, several of their products are ideally suited for preserving quilts. Due to the unprecedented increase in quilt storage requirements from collectors and museums, Archivart has now introduced the Archivart Quilt Storage Kit. Consisting of one acid-free storage box, unbuffered tissue, a quilt-lifting sling, and an instruction

Textile Conservation Products			
Barrier Paper	acid free; buffered; protective covering	7.8-8.5 pH	72x100-yards 36x100-yards
Unbuffered Tissue	neutral pH; non-buffered; interleaving	6.8-7.2 pH	24x36-yards 65x250-yards
Lining Paper	buffered; wrapping paper	minimum 8.0 pH	50x400-yards
Storage Box	acid free; folding top/bottom	7.5-8.5 pH	30x24x6-inches 60x28x5-inches

Silk quilts, like this 1880 one auctioned by Sloan's in 1996 for $900, should be examined by a professional textile conservator for storage recommendations.

booklet, this kit is an ideal "first step" for implementing a professional quilt archival storage practice.

The Department of Interior has also responded to the need for quilt conservation information. In 1993, the National Park Service, operating under the auspices of the Department of Interior, released a series of Conserve O Grams that were derived from the Curatorial Services Division of the National Park Service's Harpers Ferry Division of Conservation. These Conserve O Grams provided a set of seven guidelines for detailing the care required for the preservation of historical textiles:

- Use protective enclosures.
- Provide a stable and appropriate humidity level.
- Avoid excessive heating of objects.
- Exclude atmospheric pollutants and other contaminants.
- Provide adequate physical support for three-dimensional objects.
- Inspect objects regularly to detect and record accelerated deterioration.
- Clean objects only as necessary to remove airborne soil accumulation.

Remember that though the destructive factors of dirt, light, moisture, and acid can adversely harm your quilt, you should not feel that you have to relegate your quilt collection to a hermetically sealed chamber. In fact, consider this statement from the collector Ardis James: "What's the point of collecting quilts if you keep them folded in a closet where they can't be distinguished from bathmats?"[3]

Traditionally, crazy quilts are created from pieces or "patches" of varying fabrics that are sewn, quilted, and embroidered onto a foundation fabric layer.

Silk, satin, and taffeta are specialty fabrics that can increase the value of a crazy quilt.

Flannel, chintz, sateen, jacquard, and damask are 100 percent cotton fabrics that are commonly found on heirloom crazy quilts.

Silk-ribbon flower embellishments add an exciting dimension to the crazy quilt.

Double feather, cretan, fly, fern, herringbone, and star are examples of hand embroidery stitches that transcend function and become exotic embellishments that enhance a crazy quilt's value.

Thread color variations, as well as innovative stitch combinations, makes this crazy quilt a visual treat.

Embroidered letters, words, and initials can sometimes assist in forming a documented history of the quilt's origin. Note the fabric degradation on the light-colored silk patch along the upper right-hand edge.

A fabricated flower made from lightweight cotton flannel adds dimensional appeal to this embroidered patch.

A drawing of the 1851 James W. Edie Hopewell quilt, which failed to achieve a winning bid in 1998.

Part 1

Quilts & Prices

Attributed to the Beaver Dam, KY area, this floral quilt sold for $2,760 at a 2005 auction. (Photograph courtesy of Cowan's Auctions, Inc.)

An American circa-1925-1945 grapes pattern appliqué quilt that sold for $1,150 in 2004. (Photograph courtesy of Cowan's Auctions, Inc.)

3

Locating Antique Quilts

This tulip quilt is one of a pair of quilts that James Julia auctioned in a single lot for $862.50 in 2002. (Photograph courtesy of James D. Julia, Inc.)

One of the best (and safest) places to obtain antique quilts is through a reputable auction house. Auction houses like Butterfields, Christie's, Skinner, Sloan's, and Sotheby's are excellent representatives of reputable sources for antique quilts. Additionally, Appendix A lists several other auction houses that might offer quilts for sale. These outlets generally provide a reliable source of expertise in determining the true provenance of a sale item. This expertise is provided by a small cadre of specialists who are trained in the appraisal of antiques and collectible artifacts. In determining the merit of a memorable antique, these specialists use ten criteria for evaluating quilts:

1. Authenticity. Is it real or an intentional fake?
2. Condition. An authentic quilt in poor condition can realize a reduction in value.
3. Rarity. Unique quilts, even in poor condition, can receive a higher value than superb, commonplace varieties.
4. Provenance. The proof in the quilt can be found in its authentic documentation.
5. Historical Importance. If the provenance for a quilt

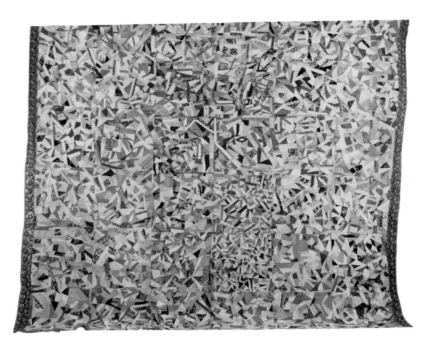

This 1839 quilt was dated via an attribution that was attached to the quilt, which was dated 1913. The winning bid for this quilt at a 1996 sale was $800. (Photograph courtesy of Sloan's).

can establish it as the work of a documented quilter, the value for the quilt will increase.

6. Size. Extraordinarily large or small quilts can command higher prices.
7. Medium. A full-size quilt will generally secure a higher price than a single quilt block.
8. Subject Matter. A terrific quilt can suffer from poor fabric selection, irregular pattern application, and/or inappropriate quilting.
9. Fashion. Antique quilts are hot. This demand drives both the market and sale prices higher.

You might want to consider quilting just one significant block from an otherwise landmark quilt. Betty Prochnow's block reproduction from the James W. Edie Hopewell quilt, which failed to achieve a winning bid at a 1998 Sotheby's auction, is as finely crafted as the 1851 original.

10. Quality. This can be a subjective criteria and specialists have to rely on their experience with a particular quilt style or quilt maker to determine the influence this will have on the quilt's price.

In spite of the competence of an auction house's specialists, all quilts sold at auction are sold "as is." This limitation is intended to prevent prospective buyers from taking any stated condition, provenance, or attribution made by the auction house as a guarantee of a quilt's worth. Any determination of a quilt's true value is therefore left in the hands of the buyer. Similarly, the sale will dictate the final worth of every quilt. Based on this limitation of warranty by the auction house, there are several points that every prospective antique quilt buyer should follow.

Estimates

Every lot in an auction from Butterfields, Christie's, Skinner, Sloan's, and Sotheby's lists a low and high estimate for each sale. These estimates are derived from the prices realized from previous sales of similar items. They are not made as claims by the auction house of the actual price that a quilt will bring during a sale; therefore, a buyer should not use them as a guide for establishing the value or worth of a quilt.

Another valuable ally in predicting the possible final sale bid for a quilt is a comprehensive pricing history for similar quilts that have been sold at auction. One of the largest, most complete quilt price history lists that has ever been published can be found in Chapter 5. Thoroughly study this chapter before you submit a bid for a known quilt type or pattern.

Occasionally, auction houses will position their staff of specialists at a presale exhibition of the sale's lots prior to the auction. These experts are available for consultation by any prospective bidder. Taking advantage of this availability is vital for understanding the basis for a quilt's estimate. Furthermore, you can obtain advice on the quilt's provenance, condition, history, and any other evaluation criteria from these specialists. This extra knowledge can go a long way towards placing an educated bid.

Bidding 101

Most auctions of quilts by Butterfields, Christie's, Skinner, Sloan's and Sotheby's are open to the public. If you plan on bidding on a particular lot, however, you must register and obtain a bidding paddle. The paddle is a large printed sign (usually round or oval in shape) that contains an identification number. This number is assigned to you upon registration prior to the sale. You will use the paddle for informing the auctioneer of your identity at the conclusion of a successful bid.

Bids can be placed in person, over the telephone, and via written bid. The bidding process, as well as the the opening bid and the proposed bid increments, is controlled by the auctioneer. Bidding wars can happen when two bidders are locked in a price competition for the same lot. You can usually avoid this type of emotional impulse bidding by establishing a value and bid limit for a particular quilt prior to the sale.

You do not have to be present during the sale to bid on any of the auction's lots. The major auction houses are always willing to accommodate absentee bidders. An absentee bidder can submit a bid in three formats:

Written. Auction sale catalogs contain absentee bid forms that can be either mailed or faxed to the auction house prior to the sale date. These forms act as your top bid limit for any lot that is offered for sale. Unfortunately, you must submit these forms blindly. In other words, you are not cognizant of the opening bid or the bid increment. Therefore, you could place a written absentee bid that is totally outrageous. After you've gained experience in auctions of antique quilts, however, you might be able to strengthen your ability to submit competitive written absentee bids.

> NOTE: There is an unwritten rule practiced by most auction houses whereby faxed and online absentee bids are not accepted from twenty-four to seventy-two hours prior to the start of the sale. Therefore, plan your absentee bidding early!

Telephone. If you would like a little more control over your bidding process, you can elect to use a telephone absentee bid. Unlike the written absentee bid, the telephone bid enables you to listen and react to the actual bidding process. There is a feeling of delay in the telephone absentee bidding process, which can generate reaction bidding, generally providing poor results for the bidder.

Proxy. You can elect to have a friend or employee attend the auction for you. This person must carry a letter providing them with the power to bid on your behalf. Once your proxy is registered for the auction, they can place bids and purchase lots exactly like any other bidder. When properly trained and educated in your bidding process, this absentee technique can be a valuable asset to the quilt collector who is unable to attend an auction.

Bidding 101

Lot Estimate	Bid Increments
$500 - $1,000	$50
$1,000 - $2,000	$100
$2,000 - $5,000	$200
$5,000 - $10,000	$500
$10,000 - $20,000	$1,000
$20,000 - $50,000	$2,000
$50,000 - $100,000	$5,000

As more and more auction houses embrace new electronic methods of bidding, the Internet is playing a pivotal role in reaching the global absentee bidder. While most auction house Web sites enable you to register for online bidding, some houses have formed alliances with eBay for enabling real-time (live) estate sales via the World Wide Web. Before you jump at this form of electronic bidding, make sure that a reputable house like Bonhams/Butterfields is sponsoring the sale and that you can virtually preview each quilt lot prior to the auction. This type of digital legwork does take time, so make sure that you begin your research effort at least three weeks before the sale date. In fact, e-mail correspondence with the auction house's textile expert can help to resolve most of your questions. Then just logon and watch the fireworks as you compete against other bidders from around the world.

Reserves

One of the least understood elements of auction bidding is the reserve. A reserve is a preestablished minimum price that the seller and the auction house have fixed to every lot in a sale. During the auction, the auctioneer will bid on behalf of the seller until this reserve is reached. After the reserve has been exceeded, the auctioneer will not continue to bid or affect the outcome of the bidding process. Generally, the reserve is determined as a percentage that is applied to all lots, and it is rarely greater than the presale low estimate.

Success

If everything goes according to your bidding strategy, when the hammer comes down, you should be the proud owner of an antique quilt. But this is just the beginning of the sequence of events that must occur before you can take your new possession home with you.

First, your winning bid is not the final price that you must pay for your quilt. Both a buyer's premium and sales tax must be added to every successful bid price. The buyer's premium is a percentage of the winning bid. For example, if the winning bid is under $50,000, a 15 percent buyer's premium is added to the quilt's actual price. For quilts priced over $50,000, the buyer's premium is reduced to 10 percent of the winning bid.

The addition of sales tax is determined by the destination of the quilt's shipment. In other words, if your state requires sales tax for mail-ordered items, then you will be assessed a sales tax charge to your winning bid. Similarly, if you pick up the quilt from one of the auction houses, then you will be charged sales tax for the state in which the auction house is located.

Regardless of the taxes and premiums, you are usually required to pay for your quilt within seven days of the conclusion of the auction. A payment invoice is sent to you along with shipping instructions. After paying the invoice, you can either elect to have your quilt shipped to you, at your expense, or pick it up from the auction house's storage facility. Some auction houses will charge a storage fee for any lots remaining in their possession longer than ten to fourteen days following the conclusion of a sale. Therefore, you should make delivery arrangements prior to attending any sale.

While shipping an antique quilt does sound like an attractive alternative to returning to the auction house for receipt of your newly acquired lot, we would recommend that you always pick up your quilt purchases in person. The fragile nature of antique fabrics necessitates proper handling and storage conditions. Oftentimes these conditions are not met by conventional package carrier services. As such, you should arm yourself with an arsenal of preservation supplies as described in Chapter 2 and carefully pack your newfound treasure for hand carrying to its new home. Remember that an antique quilt is more than a financial investment, it is a piece of history.

The Holiday

Sale 2178

December 13 & 14,

311.
Group of Early 20th Century
Women's Dresses, Knitted Wear,
Cotton Blouses, and Shoes. $200-300

Historique

312.
Paisley-backed Pieced Log Cabin
and Fan Block Pattern Quilts. $200-300

313.
Approximately Sixteen Lady's
Beaded and Mesh Purses. $150-250

314.
Four Whiting and Davis Gilt-
metal Mounted Enameled and
Painted Mesh Purses. $150-200

315.
Three French Beaded Bags,   and
an Indian bag. $175-250

316.
Lot of Women's White Cotton
Undergarments,   and Persian lamb
and mink muffs. $100-150

317.
Framed Asian Gold Embroidered
Dragon Panel and a Framed
Chinese Painted Feather Fan. $300-500

318.
Embroidered and Appliquéd
Pieced Crazy Quilt. $250-350

319.
Framed Floral Needlework Bag
with Tassel and a Flame-stitch
Purse. $400-600

320.
Five Silver and Gilt-metal
Enameled and Colored
$175-225

322.
Nine 19th and 20th Century
Women's Jackets, Coats, and
Capes, including velvet and line $250-

323.
Framed Wool Needlepoint Sai
Ship Panel. $3

324.
Brussels and Aubusson Te
Fragments and Upholster

325.
Woven Wool Paisley Sh

326.
Five Metal Mounted
Mesh Purses.

327.
Group of Textile

328.
Pieced Crazy

329.
Five Assort
Fragments

330.
Group
Vestme

331.
Seve
Me

Locate a prospective quilt in an upcoming sale from a reputable auction house. A catalog subscription to the Americana and decorative arts categories from several auction houses makes this step simple.

Do additional research on your selected lot. Some of this information might be available from the auction house's Web site.

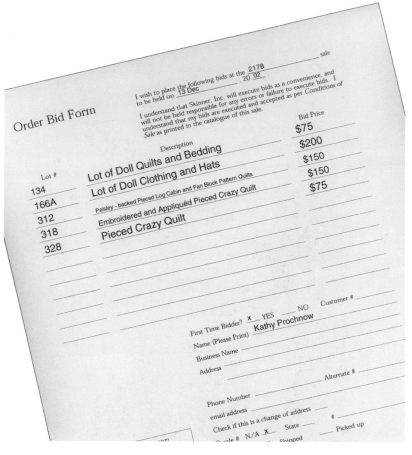

Carefully prepare and submit your bid. Most auction houses will accept faxed bids within forty-eight to twenty-four hours prior to the start of bidding.

Order Bid Form

I wish to place the following bids at the ___2178___ sale
to be held on _13 Dec_____, 20 _02_.

I understand that Skinner, Inc. will execute bids as a convenience, and
will not be held responsible for any errors or failure to execute bids. I
understand that my bids are executed and accepted as per *Conditions of
Sale* as printed in the catalogue of this sale.

Lot #	Description	Bid Price	
134	Lot of Doll Quilts and Bedding	$75	$206
166A	Lot of Doll Clothing and Hats	$200	$382
312	Paisley - backed Pieced Log Cabin and Fan Block Pattern Quilts	$150	$206
318	Embroidered and Appliquéd Pieced Crazy Quilt	$150	$176
328	Pieced Crazy Quilt	$75	$353

First Time Bidder? x YES ___ NO   Customer # _____

Name (Please Print) _Kathy Prochnow_____

Business Name _____

Address _____   Alternate # _____

Phone Number _____

email address _____

Check if this is a change of address   #_____
State _____   Picked up _____

At the conclusion of the auction, compare your bids against the winning bids.

SKINNER
Auctioneers and Appraisers of Antiques and Fine Art

INVOICE

Invoice No.	SK00005701 12/16/2002 11:40
Bidder No.	756 Sale No. 2178
Customer No.	506612

Bill To: Kathy Prochnow
319 South 13th Street
NebraskaCity NE 68410

Holiday Auction
Sale Date: 12/13/2002 10:00 AM
Session II
Sale Date: 12/13/2002 5:00 PM

Phone: 402-306-0704   Fax:

Ship To:

Lot No.	Description	Price
318	Embroidered and Appliqued Pieced Crazy Quilt.	$150.00

Total Hammer Price:	$150.00
Total Premium:	26.25
Other Charges:	0.00
Sales Tax:	0.00
Invoice Total:	$176.25

Terms: Net 7 Days

Congratulations you were a successful bidder at auction. Enclosed is a copy of your invoice. In order to expedite your shipment please complete this card and return it with your payment.

☑ Check enclosed $ _176.25_
Auction: _Holiday Auction - 2178_

SHIPPING/PICK-UP INSTRUCTIONS:
☐ Customer pickup at auction location.
☑ UPS Ground, COD, insured at full invoice value.
☐ Other, please specify _____
☐ Charge my Visa or Mastercard (Shipping charges only)
#_____ Expiration date: _____

NOTE: Shipping charges include insurance and packing/handling.

ITEMS WILL BE SHIPPED TO THE INVOICE ADDRESS UNLESS SPECIFIED BELOW:

If you have further questions regarding shipments please contact our Shipping Department at auction location.

Boston: (617) 350-5400   Bolton: (978) 779-6241

Signature: _____

SKINNER
Auctioneers and Appraisers of Antiques and Fine Art

The Heritage On The Garden, 63 Park Plaza, Boston, MA 02116 Tel: 617.350.5400 Fax: 617.350.5429
357 Main Street, Bolton, MA 01740 Tel: 978.779.6241 Fax: 978.779.5144

Success! The auction house will notify you of your winning bid. Now just complete some paperwork and make your payment.

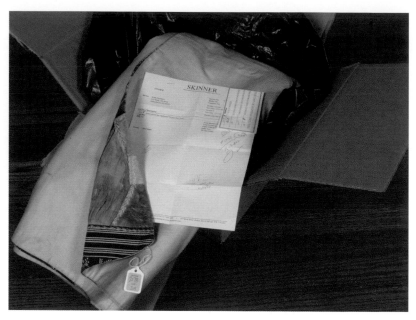

Carefully unpack your quilt lot(s) and make sure that the packing list matches your purchase order.

Within two to three weeks of the auction, your quilt lot(s) will arrive at your door.

*Behold the beauty of your new heirloom treasure . . . and immediately begin
looking for other quilts to add to your collection.*

The winning bid for this unique embroidered crazy quilt at a 2002 auction was $176.

4

Quilt Prices Realized at Auction

"My grandmother had a quilt like that one." How many times have you lamented about a potential quilt treasure that is languishing in a family member's attic? Have you ever criticized yourself for not buying a great quilt from a neighborhood garage sale? These symptoms are the early signs of developing an antique quilt collecting hobby.

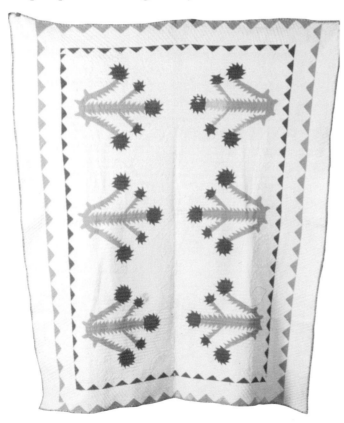

Sometimes a signature is not enough to warrant a high price. Although this quilt was signed "EM," its winning bid was $350 at a 1999 auction. (Photograph courtesy of Sloan's)

Before you rush to your local dealer with thoughts of selling your prized antique quilt for thousands of dollars, realize that any quilt is only worth the final sale price that it is able to garner. In other words, while a circa-1840 Amish quilt recently sold at auction for $10,000, it is extremely unlikely that a dealer would pay you this price for a similar quilt. So begins the murky world of price guidelines.

Price vs. Value

The prices in the price guide of Chapter 5 are derived from the actual prices realized from auctions throughout the world. However, the same quilt potentially could have commanded a higher or lower price at a different place and at a different time. You should not infer that the value for any similar quilt type or pattern is represented by the price(s) that it achieved at a particular auction. Prices can vary widely from auction house to auction house, as well as from year to year. Likewise, the true value of a quilt can be equally nebulous. Therefore, the prices cited in Chapter 5 should be used as a guide for determining future bidding tactics and not as a means for appraising the value of an antique quilt. Remember, value is in the pocketbook of the buyer, while price is in the hand of the seller.

How to Use This Guide

Begin your search for prices in this guide by locating the section heading that represents a particular quilt type or pattern. Some of these headings contain several similar types or patterns. For example, the "Star" heading lists Lone Star, Star of Bethlehem, Variable Star, Ohio Star, Feathered Star, and LeMoyne Star quilt prices. Therefore, make sure that you thoroughly study the description for each quilt price entry.

In addition to these composite headings, some headings contain a quilt type or pattern that just as easily could be cataloged in another heading. For example, a crib quilt or doll quilt could also be an Amish quilt. As such, a prudent collector searching for Amish crib quilts should study both the Amish and crib headings, as well as the price-guide heading that represents the sought-after Amish crib quilt pattern (e.g., Princess Feather or Irish Chain). It is this type of advanced compound searching that makes the price guide invaluable to every quilt collector.

In an attempt to keep the size of the price guide manageable, as well as making it informational, only a short edited description has been included with each quilt type or pattern entry. As a result, not every description provides the comprehensive information necessary to accurately judge the merit of each sold quilt's worth. These descriptions are in no way representative of the type of information that most auction houses publish for each quilt lot. On the contrary, many auction house sale catalogs feature three or four valuable pieces of quilt information for every lot sold:

1. Relative age. Unless verified by a valid provenance, the age of a quilt is limited to fifty-year estimations. For example, a quilt may be classified as late nineteenth century instead of labeled with specific year.
2. Condition. Obvious wear, tears, and/or stains are usually indicated by the auction house in its catalog description with phrases such as "some staining" or "some minor fading."
3. Size. Most quilt lots contain a statement about the quilt's overall size, stated in inches.
4. Provenance. When the provenance of a quilt is available and trustworthy, reputable auction houses will indicate the provenance. For example, "From the collection of Florence Peto, Tenafly, New Jersey."

An ideal supplement to the comprehensive price guide found in Chapter 5 is a set of catalog subscriptions from various auction houses. Almost every auction house sells either individual sale catalogs or yearly catalog subscriptions. Typically, these catalogs are sumptuous, full-color softbound books that provide superb photographs and in-depth lot descriptions for every item that is being sold at that particular auction. Unfortunately, space limitations will occasionally limit the number of photographs that a catalog can contain and therefore not every lot will be illustrated. More often than not, however, quilts obtain preferential treatment and are photographed either individually or in multi-lot display illustrations.

As a rule, quilts are featured in auctions of Americana and/or decorative arts. A frugal quilt collector would be wise in subscribing to several auction house catalogs that regularly sell antiques from these two prominent collecting categories. Luckily, most auction houses will sell you a yearly catalog subscription that is focused on their Americana and decorative art sales. Over time, these subscriptions will develop into an invaluable resource for tracing the sales and prices of quilts that are sold throughout the world. Couple this auction house reference library with the historical prices listed in Chapter 5 and you will soon find yourself bitten by the quilt-collecting bug.

Christie's auction house offers a free service for keeping you informed about upcoming quilt auctions electronically. LotFinder is an e-mail-based subscription service that enables you to enter specific keywords, your name, and e-mail address for instant notification of impending quilt sales. For example, use the keyword "quilt" and you will be notified via e-mail whenever a Christie's sale contains the word "quilt." Be forewarned, however; you might also receive messages for sales of furniture, paintings, or rugs. In fact, any sale with the word "quilt" (e.g., "a quilted lattice adorning an armoire") in a lot's description will be flagged and sent to you. You can register for LotFinder at the Christie's Web site: www.christies.com.

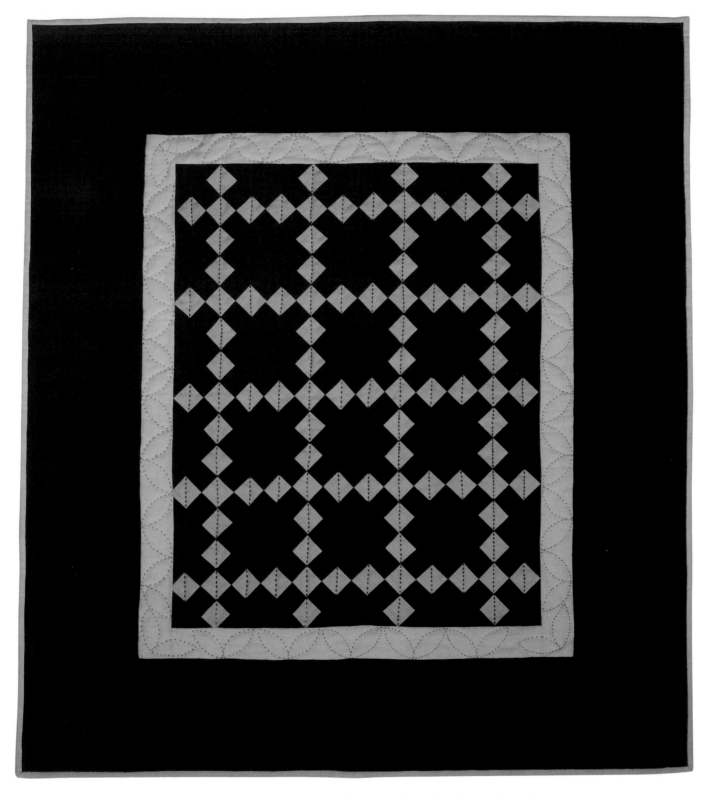

This is the author's reproduction of an Amish Irish Chain crib quilt, circa 1825, that was sold in 1994 for $920.

Cited as a circa-1900-1910 Tulip square quilt, Cowan's Auctions sold this quilt for $690 in 2004. (Photograph courtesy of Cowan's Auctions, Inc.)

Attributed to New England in the late nineteenth century, this quilt sold for $1,410 in 2004. (Photograph courtesy of Skinner, Inc. Bolton, MA)

Inscriptions can add to a quilt's value. Bearing the inscription, "C.C. SHUFELT 1853," this Patriotic quilt sold for $8,225 at a 2004 Skinner auction. (Photograph courtesy of Skinner, Inc. Bolton, MA)

5

Quilt Types & Patterns Price Guide

Each quilt type and pattern subject heading is comprised of four columnar entries. In the first column is the year of the auction when the listed quilt was sold. The second column provides an abbreviated description of the quilt lot. The third column contains the name and, where applicable, the location of the auction house. The final column lists the sale price for the quilt.

NOTE: Prices include the bid price plus a buyer's premium as established by each auction house. When attempting to convert foreign currency, use the exchange rate that was valid at the time of the sale.

1000 Pyramids

Year	Description	House	Price
2002	Signed and dated early appliqué quilt, from the Papin family	Cowan's Auctions, Inc.	$632.50

Album

Year	Description	House	Price
1988	Pieced album quilt, American, ca. 1851–1886	Skinner, Inc.	$413
1990	Album quilt, American, second half 19th century	Skinner, Inc.	$3,300
1990	Album quilt, American, mid–19th century	Skinner, Inc.	$3,080
1992	Pieced cotton presentation album quilt, Massachusetts, dated 1859	Christie's NY	$990
1992	Lovely floral appliquéd album quilt, mid- to late 19th century	James Julia	$700
1992	Pieced and appliquéd cotton album quilt top, New England, ca. 1850	Christie's NY	$2,860
1994	Pieced and appliquéd cotton Masonic album quilt, Sarah M. Snader, ca. 1850	Sotheby's NY	$2,587
1994	Pieced and appliquéd cotton summer album quilt, Cecil County, MD, dated 1854–1856	Sotheby's NY	$2,587
1995	Fine pieced cotton album quilt, ca. 1850	Sotheby's NY	$1,265

Album quilts typically command large bids. This album quilt attributed to New Jersey, circa 1850, however, was sold at a 2004 auction by Skinner for $2,115. (Photograph courtesy of Skinner, Inc. Bolton, MA)

1995	Unusual pieced and appliquéd cotton-and-chintz album quilt, signed "Lavinia Lyons," Washington, D.C., dated 1849	Sotheby's NY	$1,265
1998	Album quilt, 64" x 76"	Christie's U.K.	£207
2001	Important appliquéd album or friendship quilt, dated 1847, 110" x 110"	James Julia	$11,500
2002	Embroidered and appliquéd cotton quilt, titled "Scenes of Childhood," American, fourth quarter 19th century	Skinner, Inc.	$30,550
2004	Appliquéd quilt top with 24 blocks, three blocks signed "Rosina M. Herring Dec. b. 1847, Winifred Smith 1849," and "Hannah, Ann Robinson, Baltimore Md.," ca. 1840s, 106½" x 108"	Skinner, Inc.	$11,750

Year	Description	House	Price
2004	Forty-eight blocks depicting floral and foliate motifs, NJ, ca. 1850, 88" x 100"	Skinner, Inc.	$2,115
2004	Trapunto album quilt, probably MD, ca. 1850, approx. 96" x 96"	Sotheby's NY	$12,000
2005	Twenty-five blocks, grape-leaf border, eastern United States, ca. 1840s, 94" x 94"	Alderfer Auction Company	$1,840

Alphabet

Year	Description	House	Price
1990	Sampler by Sarah Eawoods, 1794	Christie's U.K.	£220
1992	Pieced and appliquéd cotton quilt top by Elva Smith, New York, ca. 1896	Christie's NY	$550
1998	Pieced cotton Alphabet quilt, 88" x 75"	Butterfields	$2,185

Amish

Year	Description	House	Price
1987	Fine Amish pieced cotton Star quilt, Lancaster County, PA, late 19th century	Butterfields	$3,850
1987	Good Amish appliquéd cotton crib quilt, probably OH, ca. 1930	Butterfields	$330
1987	Rare Amish pieced wool-and-cotton crib quilt made by Mrs. C. B. (Lizzy) Miller, Chavin, Holmes County, OH	Butterfields	$2,475
1987	Good Amish pieced cotton Star quilt made by Mrs. C .B. (Lizzy) Miller, Chavin, Holmes County, OH	Butterfields	$1,870
1987	Amish pieced cotton quilt, Midwestern, early 20th century	Butterfields	$2,090
1987	Good Amish pieced wool Sunshine and Shadow pattern quilt, initialed "K. S.," PA, early 20th century	Butterfields	$3,575
1989	Amish quilt Baby Block variant in purples with feather stitching, 80" x 80"	Robert Eldred Co.	$495
1989	Amish quilt open squares made from triangles on a green ground, 80" x 80"	Robert Eldred Co.	$385
1990	Pieced Amish quilt	Christie's NY	$176
1990	Amish homespun crib quilt, 19th century	Christie's NY	$77
1990	Amish pieced wool crepe quilted coverlet, probably Midwestern, second quarter 20th century	Christie's NY	$990
1990	Amish pieced cotton-and-wool quilted coverlet, Lancaster County, PA	Christie's NY	$1,540
1991	Amish Diamond pattern quilt with blue ground	Northeast Auctions	$1,200
1991	Amish Star of Bethlehem quilt	Northeast Auctions	$600
1991	Amish pieced and appliquéd quilted cotton coverlet, probably OH, ca. 1920	Christie's NY	$1,650
1991	Amish pieced cotton quilted coverlet, Lancaster County, PA, ca. 1930	Christie's NY	$880

Year	Description	Auction House	Price
1991	Amish pieced wool-and-crepe quilted coverlet, Lancaster County, PA, ca. 1940	Christie's NY	$935
1991	Two Amish pieced cotton quilted coverlets, probably OH, ca. 1930	Christie's NY	$605
1991	Amish pieced cotton quilted coverlet, probably Midwestern, ca. 1930	Christie's NY	$77
1991	Amish pieced wool quilted coverlet, Lancaster County, PA, ca. 1920	Christie's NY	$2,750
1991	Amish pieced wool quilted coverlet, Lancaster County, PA, ca. 1920	Christie's NY	$2,200
1991	Amish quilted wool coverlet, initialed "A. S.," probably Lancaster County, PA, ca. 1925	Christie's NY	$2,640
1991	Amish pieced cotton quilted coverlet, PA, ca. 1930	Christie's NY	$3,850
1991	Amish quilted wool-and-wool crepe coverlet, probably Lancaster County, PA, ca. 1940	Christie's NY	$2,200
1991	Amish pieced and appliquéd quilted cotton coverlet, probably OH, ca. 1920, 89" x 72"	Christie's NY	$1,650
1991	Amish pieced cotton-and-wool quilted coverlet, probably Holmes County, OH, 1908	Christie's NY	$4,400
1991	Amish pieced cotton crib quilt, Midwestern, 1920-1940	Christie's NY	$990
1991	Amish pieced cotton crib quilt, Midwestern, ca. 1910	Christie's NY	$2,860
1991	Amish pieced cotton quilted coverlet, Lancaster County, PA, ca. 1930, 65" x 88"	Christie's NY	$880
1991	Amish pieced wool-and-cotton quilted coverlet, probably OH, dated 1914	Christie's NY	$3,300
1991	Two Amish pieced cotton quilted coverlets, the first probably Ohio, 68" x 88", the second quilt from Mifflin County, PA, 66" x 72", both ca. 1930,	Christie's NY	$605
1991	Amish quilt, 20th century	Skinner, Inc.	$253
1991	Amish pieced cotton quilted coverlet, probably Midwestern, ca. 1930, 82" x 82"	Christie's NY	$77
1991	Antique Amish patchwork quilt in Drunken Path pattern, PA, 84" x 76"	Sloan's DC	$303
1991	Amish pieced cotton quilted coverlet, western PA or OH, ca. 1920	Christie's NY	$3,080
1991	Antique Amish patchwork quilt in Nine Patch pattern, PA, 84" x 66"	Sloan's DC	$190
1991	Amish crib quilt, PA, early 20th century, 33" x 28"	Sloan's DC	$28
1991	Rare Amish cotton quilted coverlet, Lancaster County, PA, ca, 1920	Christie's NY	$5,500
1991	Amish pieced quilt, probably Lancaster County, PA, late 19th/early 20th century	Skinner, Inc.	$1,540
1991	Pieced Amish quilt	Christie's NY	$77
1992	Amish cotton quilted coverlet, Midwestern, ca. 1930	Christie's NY	$1,045
1992	Fine Amish crib quilt, probably OH, early 20th century	James Julia	$550

1992	Amish pieced wool-and-cotton quilted coverlet, Lancaster County, PA, ca. 1920	Christie's NY	$3,850
1992	Amish pieced cotton quilted coverlet, initialed "B," OH, dated 1916	Christie's NY	$4,950
1992	Amish pieced wool-and-cotton quilted coverlet, Lancaster County, PA, ca. 1925	Christie's NY	$3,520
1992	Amish pieced wool-and-cotton embroidered and quilted coverlet, Topeka, IN, dated 1899	Christie's NY	$7,700
1992	Amish pieced wool-and-cotton quilted coverlet, Lancaster County, PA, ca. 1930	Christie's NY	$1,650
1992	Amish pieced wool-and-cotton quilted coverlet, Lancaster County, PA, ca. 1850	Christie's NY	$14,850
1992	Amish quilt in Tumbling Block pattern, initialed "E. L. S.," dated 1963, 76" x 86½"	James Julia	$500
1992	Pieced and appliquéd Amish cotton quilted crib quilt, 42" x 69"	Christie's NY	$385
1992	Amish quilted and appliquéd cotton coverlet, worked in the Jacob's Bars pattern, American	Christie's NY	$165
1992	Amish pieced cotton quilted coverlet, American, ca. 1930, rectangular	Christie's NY	$660
1992	Rare Amish or Mennonite pieced cotton quilted coverlet, Martin M. Lichty, Lancaster County, PA, 1879	Christie's NY	$6,050
1992	Amish cotton-and-wool quilted coverlet, American, ca. 1930	Christie's NY	$2,860
1992	Amish pieced wool-and-cotton quilted coverlet, Lancaster County, PA, ca. 1910	Christie's NY	$6,600
1992	Amish pieced cotton-and-wool quilted and embroidered coverlet, IN, ca. 1930	Christie's NY	$1,540
1992	Pieced Amish quilt, PA or OH, late 19th/early 20th century	Skinner, Inc.	$2,750
1994	Amish pieced cotton Bar quilt	Sotheby's NY	$4,312
1995	Pieced and appliquéd cotton quilt, American	Sotheby's NY	$460
1995	Pieced calico Split Bar quilt	Sotheby's NY	$805
1995	Pieced cotton Amish quilt, ca. 1940	Sotheby's NY	$1,150
1996	Amish pieced cotton quilt	Sloan's DC	$1,100
1998	Amish pieced cotton Sawtooth Diamond in the Square quilt, 80" x 82"	Butterfields	$3,737.50
1998	Amish pieced Bar quilt, Lancaster County, PA late 19th/early 20th century	Sotheby's NY	$3,737
1998	Amish pieced Diamond in the Square quilt, 78" x 76"	Sotheby's NY	$1,725
1999	American calico cotton quilt, 79" x 90"	Sloan's DC	$65
1999	Amish wool and cotton Bars quilted coverlet	Christie's NY	$2,820
1999	Amish wool and cotton Diamond in the Square quilted coverlet	Christie's NY	$2,350
1999	Amish wool and cotton Diamond in the Square quilted coverlet	Christie's NY	$5,640
1999	Amish wool and cotton Sunshine and Shadow quilted coverlet	Christie's NY	$3,055
1999	Fine Amish pieced Roman Stripe quilt, Holmes County, OH, ca. 1900	Sotheby's NY	$3,162
1999	Unusual pieced cotton Amish quilt, OH, ca. 1930	Sotheby's NY	$1,150

A breathtaking Baltimore Album quilt, circa 1840s, was sold by Skinner in 2004 for $11,750. (Photograph courtesy of Skinner, Inc. Bolton, MA)

2001	Amish cotton T Blocks and Bars quilt, ca. 1920	Butterfields	$1,116.25
2001	Amish cotton Sunshine and Shadow quilt, ca. 1950	Butterfields	$940
2002	Amish child's pieced quilt, 20th century	Cowan's Auctions, Inc.	$161
2002	Blue, red, and gray with black background, 77" x 67½"	Ken Farmer Auctions & Appraisals, LLC	$1,610
2002	Blue, rust, and pink on a rust background, with initials in quilting, dated January 8, 1913, 79½" x 57"	Ken Farmer Auctions & Appraisals, LLC	$632.50

2002	Red on black, 81" x 65½"	Ken Farmer Auctions & Appraisals, LLC	$690
2003	Quilt, 84" x 72"	Ken Farmer Auctions & Appraisals, LLC	$150
2004	Bar pattern quilt	Skinner, Inc.	$293.75
2004	Floating Diamond pattern quilt	Skinner, Inc.	$293.75
2005	Made by Esther Williams, Holmes County, OH, ca. 1940, 76" x 70½"	Pook & Pook, Inc.	$1,020
2005	Mennonite appliqué quilt with wreath quilting, Lancaster County, PA, 86" x 91"	Pook & Pook, Inc.	$1,560
2005	Mennonite, early 20th century, 7' x 7'	Pook & Pook, Inc.	$805
2005	York County, PA, early 20th century, 71" x 83"	Pook & Pook, Inc.	$460

Broderie Perse

Year	Description	House	Price
1999	Broderie Perse coverlet	Christie's U.K.	£517
1999	Broderie Perse quilt	Christie's U.K.	£460

Baltimore Album

Year	Description	House	Price
1989	Extremely rare and important 16-panel Baltimore Album quilt	Richard Bourne Co.	$20,350
1991	Fine pieced and appliquéd cotton quilted coverlet attributed to Mary Brown, Calvert, MD, 1852	Christie's NY	$49,500
1995	Fine pieced and appliquéd Baltimore Album quilt, dated March 4, 1841	Sotheby's NY	$5,462
1998	Extremely fine and rare appliquéd and embroidered Baltimore-style album quilt, signed Mary Foster and Elizabeth Holland	Sotheby's NY	$8,625
1998	Fine pieced and appliquéd Baltimore Album quilt, ca. 1860	Sotheby's NY	$8,050
2000	Baltimore Album quilt	Pook & Pook, Inc.	$24,200
2004	Baltimore Album quilt attributed to Hannah Foote, Baltimore, MD, ca. 1860, approx. 103" by 104"	Sotheby's NY	$72,000
2005	A Baltimore pieced cotton quilt, ca. 1850, 88" square	Sloan's DC	$550

Basket, Flower Basket, Basket of Lilies, Cactus Basket

Year	Description	House	Price
1987	Silk patchwork quilt, 19th century	Robert Eldred Co.	$99
1987	Antique appliquéd quilt	Robert Eldred Co.	$165
1988	Two patchwork quilts, 20th century, 97" x 90"	Skinner, Inc.	$413
1989	Stuffed work crib quilt, possibly southern United States, mid-19th century	Skinner, Inc.	$357.50
1990	Pieced and appliquéd quilt, American, second half 19th century	Skinner, Inc.	$990
1990	Appliquéd quilt, possibly PA, dated 1856	Skinner, Inc.	$770

This Basket pattern quilt, circa 1900, sold for $1,527.50 in 2004.
(Photograph courtesy of Skinner, Inc. Bolton, MA)

1990	Flower Basket	Christie's U.K.	£418
1990	Flower Basket	Christie's U.K.	£209
1990	Two white-on-white quilted cotton coverlets, American, mid–19th century	Christie's NY	$154
1991	Pieced linsey-woolsey quilt, American, late 18th/early 19th century	Skinner, Inc.	$495

This exquisite Baltimore Flower Basket pattern quilt, attributed to Elizabeth Livingston, Wilmington, Pennsylvania, 1807, commanded a winning bid of $9,987.50 at a 2004 Skinner auction. (Photograph courtesy of Skinner, Inc. Bolton, MA)

1991	Pieced worsted quilt, American, early 19th century	Skinner, Inc.	$550
1991	White-on-white stuffed cotton crib quilt, probably American, 1790–1810	Christie's NY	$2,640
1991	Two appliquéd quilts with red-and-green calico Basket motif and a scalloped edge, American	Leslie Hindman, Inc.	$385
1991	Pieced and appliquéd cotton quilted coverlet, MD, ca. 1810	Christie's NY	$2,640
1991	Pieced quilt, American, late 19th/early 20th century	Skinner, Inc.	$176
1991	Pieced and appliquéd cotton quilted coverlet, Mary Swartz, Shiloh, OH, 1853	Christie's NY	$5,500

1991	Amish pieced cotton crib quilt, Midwestern, 1920-1940	Christie's NY	$990
1992	Pieced and appliquéd cotton quilted coverlet	Christie's NY	$220
1992	Pieced and appliquéd quilted cotton coverlet, American, 20th century	Christie's NY	$275
1992	Pieced and appliquéd cotton quilted coverlet, SC, ca. 1830	Christie's NY	$4,400
1992	Amish pieced wool-and-cotton quilted coverlet, Lancaster County, PA, ca. 1920	Christie's NY	$3,850
1992	Pieced and appliquéd cotton quilted coverlet, American, ca. 1930	Christie's NY	$88
1992	Amish cotton quilted coverlet, Midwestern, ca. 1930	Christie's NY	$1,045
1992	Quilt, 19th century, 86" x 86"	James Julia	$650
1992	Pieced and appliquéd cotton quilted coverlet	Christie's NY	$220
1992	American appliqué quilt with basket of flowers	Northeast Auctions	$375
1992	Amish pieced wool-and-cotton quilted coverlet, Lancaster County, PA, ca. 1910	Christie's NY	$6,600
1995	Fine pieced and appliquéd cotton quilt initialed "M. E. S."	Sotheby's NY	$805
1995	Pieced blue-and-white calico-and-cotton Flower Basket quilt	Sotheby's NY	$920
1999	Basket appliqué quilt	Christie's U.K.	£149
1999	Basket of Lilies appliqué quilt attributed to Mrs. Morgan of Tennessee	Christie's U.K.	£207
1999	Cactus Basket variation quilt	Christie's U.K.	£345
1999	Group of three pieced and appliquéd cotton quilted coverlets	Christie's NY	$115
1999	Pieced and appliquéd cotton quilted coverlet	Christie's NY	$863
1999	Pieced and appliquéd cotton quilted coverlet	Christie's NY	$1,380
2005	Late 19th century, 71" x 87"	Pook & Pook, Inc.	$431
2005	Late 19th century, 81" x 68"	Pook & Pook, Inc.	$240
2005	Late 19th century, 83" x 74"	Pook & Pook, Inc.	$345
2005	NY, late 19th century, 73" x 75"	Pook & Pook, Inc.	$230
2005	Yellow and pink outlined by blue bands, 79" x 78"	Alderfer Auction Company	$207

Bear's Paw

Year	Description	House	Price
1999	Quilt	Christie's U.K.	£207
2001	Signatures and dates 1880s-1890s	Winter Associates	$302.50
2002	From the hand of or property of Nina Wilson Creel, who lived in the "Seven Mile House," Davisville, WV, 64"x 77"	Ken Farmer Auctions & Appraisals, LLC	$115
2005	Early 20th century, 80" x 82"	Pook & Pook, Inc.	$450

Carolina Lily

Year	Description	House	Price
1998	Pieced and appliquéd cotton and trapunto North Carolina Lily quilt	Butterfields	$1,092.50

Carolina Lily pattern.

Year	Description	House	Price
2002	Blue on white background from the hand of or property of Nina Wilson Creel, who lived in the "Seven Mile House," Davisville, WV, 66" x 84"	Ken Farmer Auctions & Appraisals, LLC	$460
2005	IA, ca. 1930, 74" x 90"	Cowan's Auctions, Inc.	$431.25
2005	From the Zeigler family, VA, late 19th century, 90" x 96"	Pook & Pook, Inc.	$690

Chimney Sweep

Year	Description	House	Price
1998	Pieced cotton quilt	Butterfields	$431.25

Crazy

Year	Description	House	Price
1986	Silk crazy quilt, American, 19th century, 82" x 74"	Robert Eldred Co.	$176
1987	Victorian pieced and embroidered crazy quilt, 19th century	Butterfields	$412.50
1988	Victorian and satin patchwork crazy quilt, American, 19th century	Skinner, Inc.	$660

1988	American pieced crazy quilt	Butterfields	$385
1988	Unusual Japanese American pieced crazy quilt, 19th century	Butterfields	$192.50
1989	Doll crazy quilt	Butterfields	$44
1989	Victorian crazy quilt, 19th century, 69" x 68"	Skinner, Inc.	$193
1989	Patchwork crazy quilt, 1894	Skinner, Inc.	$303
1990	Crazy quilt and two shams, American, late 19th century	Skinner, Inc.	$440
1990	Embroidered and beaded silk-and-velvet crazy crib quilt, American, 1891	Christie's NY	$880
1990	Pieced, appliquéd, and embroidered silk-and-velvet crazy quilt, American, late 19th century, 70" x 70"	Skinner, Inc.	$1,045
1990	Pieced quilt, America, late 19th century	Skinner, Inc.	$550
1991	Pieced and embroidered silk-and-velvet coverlet American, ca. 1885	Christie's NY	$2,090
1991	Fine silk crazy quilt, late 19th century	Robert Eldred Co.	$248
1991	Antique hand-sewn crazy quilt, dated 1910	Robert Eldred Co.	$55
1991	Pieced and embroidered wool crazy quilt, signed "MLB 1896," American, 76" x 76"	Skinner, Inc.	$302.50
1991	Crazy quilt, 19th century	Robert Eldred Co.	$110
1991	American felt crazy quilt; together with another crazy quilt	Leslie Hindman	$110
1991	Antique hand-sewn crazy quilt, monogrammed "S" in center, 71" x 75"	Robert Eldred Co.	$33
1991	Pieced silk crib quilt, American, 1880-1900	Christie's NY	$440
1992	Pieced and embroidered silk-and-velvet crazy quilt, American, dated 1885	Skinner, Inc.	$330
1992	Silk-and-velvet embroidered, pieced, and appliquéd contained crazy quilt, American, late 19th century	Christie's NY	$3,300
1992	Watercolor, embroidered silk-and-velvet crazy quilt, American, initialed "H. N. C.," dated 1887	Christie's NY	$330
1992	Pieced, appliquéd, and embroidered silk-and-velvet contained crazy quilt, American, ca. 1890	Christie's NY	$11,000
1992	Pieced and embroidered silk-and-velvet coverlet with 56 blocks of contained crazy quilt pattern	Christie's NY	$330
1992	Appliquéd and embroidered silk-and-cotton crazy quilt, American, 1902	Christie's NY	$110
1992	Pieced and appliquéd crazy quilt, American, ca. 1930	Christie's NY	$715
1996	American pieced and appliquéd crazy quilt	Sloan's DC	$950
1996	Early American pieced cotton crazy quilt	Sloan's DC	$800
1998	Pieced cotton crazy quilt, 70" x 78"	Butterfields	$862.50
1998	Very fine silk crazy quilt, illustrated on cover of 1992 Hallmark calendar	Butterfields	$12,650
1998	Crazy patchwork coverlet, 46" x 64"	Christie's U.K.	£80
1998	Crazy patchwork coverlet, 66" x 62"	Christie's U.K.	£207
1998	Crazy patchwork coverlet, 82" x 80"	Christie's U.K.	£299
1998	Fine and rare appliquéd and embroidered pieced crazy quilt, 80" x 68"	Sotheby's NY	$6,325

Year	Description	House	Price
1998	Fine central Medallion crazy quilt	Sotheby's NY	$4,600
1999	Pieced velvet crazy quilt	Christie's NY	$115
2000	Three quilts, late 19th/early 20th century	Winter Associates	$55
2002	Crazy patchwork coverlet with the central date 1888	Christie's U.K.	£587
2002	Silk pieces, embroidered, ca. 1890, 59" x 59"	Winter Associates	$440
2002	Embroidered and appliquéd pieced crazy quilt	Skinner, Inc.	$353
2002	Sewn with a herringbone stitch, late 19th century, 87" x 66"	Winter Associates	$60.50
2002	Pieced crazy quilt	Skinner, Inc.	$176
2002	Three 20th century quilts, 93" x 75"; 104" x 87"; one panel is embroidered "Pearl Christmas 1905," 93" x 93"	Winter Associates	$165
2002	Two pieced cotton patchwork quilt tops; one silk crazy quilt top	Winter Associates	$330
2002	Victorian crazy quilt, last quarter 19th century	Butterfields	$1,292.50
2003	Lot of three, all 19th century; 64" x 77"; cotton crazy quilt, 78" x 85"; 76" x 93"	Cowan's Auctions, Inc.	$86.25
2004	Black border, multiple stitching patterns, 19th century, 55" x 72"	Winter Associates	$448
2004	Mixed fibers, 19th century	Winter Associates	$39.20
2004	Marked "Our Lady C. T. A. and B. Society, Rockville Conn. Organized: August 29, 1888," monogrammed "P. T. B.," 19th century, 6' x 6' 3"	Winter Associates	$112
2004	Signed, 19th century, 66" x 56"	Winter Associates	$168
2004	Signed with fan designs in silks, velvets, and satins, initialed "F. B. W.," 19th century	Winter Associates	$336
2004	Applied lace border, 19th century, 4' 7" x 6' 4"	Winter Associates	$280
2004	Embroidered velvet crazy quilt, PA	Skinner, Inc.	$381.88
2004	Jewel-tone velvets with calico backing, 67½" x 80"	Alderfer Auction Company	$805
2004	Late 19th century	Pook & Pook, Inc.	$144
2004	Patches of many fabrics and featuring several photographic silks, 67" x 58"	Alderfer Auction Company	$402.50
2004	Runner with embroidered joints and decoration, 43" x 18½"	Alderfer Auction Company	$161
2004	Silk-embroidered bed cover, dated in one corner "1884," 72" x 62", maker of quilt Emily Sprague, Mattewan, NY	Robert S. Brunk Auction Services, Inc.	$5,000
2004	Velvet and satin multicolor fabrics, seams embroidered, 79" x 81"	Alderfer Auction Company	$690
2005	Quilt, Berks County, PA, dated 1897, 77" x 80"	Pook & Pook, Inc.	$316
2005	Includes two political ribbons depicting Cleveland-Hendricks and Blaine-Logan (election of 1884), 61" square	Cowan's Auctions, Inc.	$480
2005	Victorian with applied green border and lace overlay, 67" x 77"	Winter Associates	$224
2005	Victorian with center Star design, 68" x 72"	Winter Associates	$252

Crib

Year	Description	House	Price
1987	Good Amish appliquéd cotton crib quilt, probably OH, ca. 1930	Butterfields	$330

1987	Rare Amish pieced wool-and-cotton crib quilt made by Mrs. C. B. (Lizzy) Miller, Chavin, Holmes County, OH	Butterfields	$2,475
1988	Rare baby's crib quilt, ca. 19th century, 41" x 33"	Richard Bourne Co.	$550
1988	Two patchwork quilts, late 19th century	William Doyle Galleries, NY	$330
1989	Stuffed work quilt, possibly southern United States, mid-19th century	Skinner, Inc.	$357.50
1989	Appliqué crib quilt, probably NY, ca. 1915	Skinner, Inc.	$522.50
1989	Lot of three crib quilts: one in poor condition, two in good condition	Richard Bourne Co.	$121
1990	Amish homespun crib quilt, 19th century	Christie's NY	$77
1990	Embroidered and beaded silk-and-velvet crazy crib quilt, American, 1891	Christie's NY	$880
1990	Pieced and appliquéd two-sided cotton crib quilt, American, late 19th/early 20th century	Christie's NY	$385
1990	Amish homespun crib quilt, 19th century	Christie's NY	$77
1991	Amish pieced cotton crib quilt, Midwestern, ca. 1910	Christie's NY	$2,860
1991	White-on-white corded cotton crib quilt, probably American, 1790-1810	Christie's NY	$1,870
1991	Amish crib quilt, PA, early 20th century, 33" x 28"	Sloan's DC	$28
1991	Appliquéd crib quilt, probably PA, late 19th/early 20th century	Skinner, Inc.	$165
1991	Pieced and appliquéd cotton crib quilt, American, mid-19th century	Christie's NY	$550
1991	Pieced silk crib quilt, American, 1880-1900	Christie's NY	$440
1991	White-on-white stuffed cotton crib quilt, probably American, 1790-1810	Christie's NY	$2,640
1991	Amish pieced cotton crib quilt, Midwestern, 1920-1940	Christie's NY	$990
1991	Fine silk crazy quilt, late 19th century	Robert Eldred Co.	$248
1992	Pieced and appliquéd Amish cotton quilted crib quilt, 42" x 69"	Christie's NY	$385
1992	Pieced and appliquéd quilted cotton crib coverlet, OH, 19th century	Christie's NY	$220
1992	Fine Amish crib quilt, probably OH, ca. early 20th century	James Julia	$550
1992	Pair of double-woven dark and light blue jacquard coverlets attributed to David Harring, Bergen County, NJ, 1838	Christie's NY	$2,200
1992	Crib quilt in the Flying Geese pattern, late 19th/early 20th century	James Julia	$400
1994	Pieced cotton crib quilt, New England, mid-19th century	Sotheby's NY	$805
1994	Pieced cotton Flying Geese crib quilt, New England, ca. 1860	Sotheby's NY	$1,955
1994	Pieced cotton Star crib quilt, New England, 1890-1900	Sotheby's NY	$805
1998	Quilted cotton crib quilt, inscribed "KITKA"	Butterfields	$126.50
1998	Pieced cotton Baby Block child's quilt, American, late 19th/early 20th century	Sotheby's NY	$172
1998	Two pieced cotton children's quilts, American, late 19th/early 20th century	Sotheby's NY	$1,265
1998	Two pieced cotton crib quilts, PA, 19th century	Sotheby's NY	$575
1999	Cotton crib quilt	Christie's NY	$1,035

Year	Description	House	Price
1999	Pieced and appliquéd cotton quilted crib quilt, signed "Irene Allen"	Christie's NY	$230
2002	Amish child's pieced quilt, 20th century	Cowan's Auctions, Inc.	$161
2002	Amish quilt in black and white on purple with borders, 42½" x 36"	Ken Farmer Auctions & Appraisals, LLC	$632.50
2002	Amish quilt in blues and whites on a green background with tan and blue borders, 52½" x 42½"	Ken Farmer Auctions & Appraisals, LLC	$488.75
2002	Three quilts: ca. 1850, "A. Moses" ink inscription, 43" x 43"; ca. 1840, 74½" x 84"; ca. 1860, 53½" x 26"	Winter Associates	$412.50
2003	Amish, black-and-green border, 70" x 36"	Ken Farmer Auctions & Appraisals, LLC	$200
2003	Amish quilt with violet borders enclosing blue rectangular color blocks, 56" x 40"	Ken Farmer Auctions & Appraisals, LLC	$500
2003	Four-Patch, 19th century, 36" x 37"	Skinner, Inc.	$528.75
2003	Lot of four; includes a child's Double Nine Patch pattern, ca. 1860-80, 39" x 41½"	Cowan's Auctions, Inc.	$201.25
2004	Predominantly pink floral pattern center, early 19th century, 56" x 51"	Skinner, Inc.	$381.88
2004	Log Cabin with burgundy, cream, and browns, 39½" x 37"	Winter Associates	$336
2004	Log Cabin with purples and reds, 4' 10" x 3' 8"	Winter Associates	$56
2004	Ring of peach-colored flowers, 53" x 37"	Winter Associates	$112
2004	Three quilts: one white, one pink and white, and one multicolored	Winter Associates	$168
2004	Tumbling Blocks with black velvet and silks, 52" x 40"	Winter Associates	$84
2005	Geometric crib quilt	Skinner, Inc.	$117.50
2005	Courthouse Step, dated in pencil on back, most in 1892, late 19th century, 38½" x 56"	Winter Associates	$224

Delectable Mountains

Year	Description	House	Price
1998	Pieced cotton Delectable Mountains quilt, early 20th century	Butterfields	$862.50
1998	Pieced cotton Delectable Mountains quilt	Butterfields	$517.50

Doll

Year	Description	House	Price
1988	Two pieced cotton or calico doll's quilts, American, ca. 1920	Butterfields	$44
1988	Three patchwork doll quilts	Butterfields	$66
1988	American pieced cotton Shoo-Fly pattern quilt, Laura West, Carthage, MO, ca. 1897	Butterfields	$440

1988	American pieced cotton Bow Tie pattern quilt, Laura West, Carthage, MO, ca. 1897	Butterfields	$440
1988	Patchwork quilt	Butterfields	$55
1988	American pieced cotton Monkey Wrench pattern quilt, Laura West, Carthage, MO, ca. 1897	Butterfields	$192.50
1988	Two embroidered cotton quilts, American	Butterfields	$522.50
1988	Pieced cotton quilt, American	Butterfields	$385
1988	Pieced cotton Flying Geese pattern quilt, American, 19th century	Butterfields	$385
1989	Doll crazy quilt	Butterfields	$44
1989	Two doll-size patchwork quilts, late 19th century, 25¾" x 21"	Skinner, Inc.	$412.50
1989	Doll quilts	Butterfields	$55
1989	Child's cotton quilt and four boxed paper toys, late 18th/early 19th century	Skinner, Inc.	$715
1989	Doll quilts	Butterfields	$22
1990	Five composition dolls and two doll quilts, 1920-1930s	Skinner, Inc.	$193
1991	Group of dolls, doll clothing, and bedding, 20th century	Skinner, Inc.	$825
1992	Piecework doll's quilt in the Broken Dishes pattern, 19th century	James Julia	$300
2000	Three quilts, late 19th/early 20th century	Winter Associates	$55
2002	Eight doll quilts and bedding, late 19th century and 20th century	Skinner, Inc.	$206
2002	Doll clothing, hats, and quilts	Skinner, Inc.	$382
2003	A blue-painted doll bed; mattress and quilt	Christie's NY	$239
2004	Three quilts: one white, one pink and white, and one multicolored	Winter Associates	$168

Double Wedding Ring

Year	Description	House	Price
1989	Appliquéd quilt in Double Wedding Ring pattern, 8' 2" square	Richard A. Bourne	$275
1990	Double Wedding Ring patchwork quilt	Christie's U.K.	£77
1990	Double Wedding Ring patchwork quilt	Christie's U.K.	£286
1990	Double Wedding Ring quilt, 78" square	Christie's U.K.	£242
1991	Double Wedding Ring pattern quilt	Dunning's	$130
1992	Decorated doll's hooded cradle with Double Wedding Ring quilt	James Julia	$300
1995	Three pieced cotton quilts, American	Sotheby's NY	$1,380
1999	Cotton quilt, American, 7' 7" x 6' 2"	Sloan's DC	$300
2002	Multicolored cotton quilt from Nina Wilson Creel, who lived in the "Seven Mile House," Davisville, WV, 73" x 73"	Ken Farmer Auctions & Appraisals, LLC	$172.50
2002	Lilac and floral print with green border, early 20th century, 78" x 78"	Winter Associates	$220
2005	Cream field, 20th century, 79" x 82"	Winter Associates	$75

2005	Two Wedding Ring pattern quilts; blue border quilt 8' 2" x 6' 9"; pink border quilt 6' 8" x 5' 10"	Auctions by the Bay	$120

Dresden Plate

Year	Description	House	Price
1992	Dresden Plate quilt, American	Northeast Auctions	$300
1998	Dresden Plate variation quilt, 64" x 84"	Christie's U.K.	£368
1998	Dresden Plate variation quilt, 68" x 78"	Christie's U.K.	£172
1998	Pieced cotton Dresden Plate quilt, 80" x 64"	Butterfields	$172.50
1999	Dresden Plate quilt, 76" x 80"	Christie's U.K.	£149
1999	Dresden Plate variation quilt	Christie's U.K.	£253
2002	Multicolored pastel print fabric on white from Nina Wilson Creel, who lived in the "Seven Mile House," Davisville, WV, 72" x 89"	Ken Farmer Auctions & Appraisals, LLC	$115
2004	Pastels and florals on a green field with a lavender border strip, early 20th century, 66" x 83"	Winter Associates	$84

Drunkard's Path

Year	Description	House	Price
1992	Drunkard's Path blue-and-white quilt	Northeast Auctions	$325
1995	Pieced calico Drunkard's Path quilt, American	Sotheby's NY	$517
1998	Pieced cotton Drunkard's Path quilt, dated 1920	Butterfields	$546.25
1998	Pieced cotton Drunkard's Path pattern quilt, probably PA, mid-19th century	Sotheby's NY	$575
2002	Three quilts: ca. 1850, "A. Moses" ink inscription, 43" x 43"; ca. 1840, 74½" x 84"; ca. 1860, 53½" x 26"	Winter Associates	$412.50
2004	Red on white with solid red border, 78" x 65"	Winter Associates	$140

Embroidered

Year	Description	House	Price
1987	Victorian pieced and embroidered crazy quilt, 19th century	Butterfields	$412.50
1987	Unusual Mennonite pieced and embroidered cotton quilt, Midwestern, dated 1907	Butterfields	$1,870
1987	American pieced cotton Crown of Thorns pattern quilt, probably Midwestern, ca. 1920	Butterfields	$522.50
1987	Pieced cotton-and-calico quilt, American, 20th century	Butterfields	$302.50
1987	Unusual appliquéd cotton sampler quilt, inscribed "Cora Erwin," American, ca. 1920	Butterfields	$467.50
1988	Pieced crazy quilt, American	Butterfields	$385
1988	Victorian and satin patchwork crazy quilt, American, 19th century	Skinner, Inc.	$660
1988	Two embroidered cotton quilts, American	Butterfields	$522.50

The winning bid for this Drunkard's Path circa-1920-1930 quilt in 2004 was $488.75. (Photograph courtesy of Cowan's Auctions, Inc.)

1988	Group of four patchwork quilts	William Doyle Galleries	$660
1989	Patchwork crazy quilt, 1894	Skinner, Inc.	$303
1989	Victorian crazy quilt, 19th century, 69" x 68"	Skinner, Inc.	$193
1990	Embroidered and beaded silk-and-velvet crazy crib quilt, American, 1891	Christie's NY	$880
1990	Appliquéd and embroidered quilt, American, 20th century	Skinner, Inc.	$1,760
1990	Patchwork and appliqué coverlet	Christie's U.K.	£55
1990	Hexagon patchwork coverlet	Christie's U.K.	£440
1990	Pieced, appliquéd, and embroidered silk-and-velvet crazy quilt, American, late 19th century, 70" x 70"	Skinner, Inc.	$1,045
1990	Framed patchwork quilt	Christie's U.K.	£495
1991	Pieced and embroidered silk quilt, American, late 19th century	Skinner, Inc.	$495
1991	Pieced, appliquéd, and embroidered Civil War quilt, NY, 1867, 100" x 88"	Sotheby's NY	$240,000
1991	Pieced silk crib quilt, American, 1880-1900	Christie's NY	$440
1991	Pieced and embroidered wool crazy quilt, signed "MLB 1896," American, 76" x 76"	Skinner, Inc.	$302.50
1991	Embroidered worsted wool coverlet, American, late 18th/early 19th century	Skinner, Inc.	$522.50
1991	Pieced and embroidered silk-and-velvet coverlet, American, ca. 1885	Christie's NY	$2,090
1991	Appliqué quilt made by Eliza Crane Smith, MA, 1884	Skinner, Inc.	$825
1992	Pieced and embroidered silk-and-velvet crazy quilt, American, dated 1885	Skinner, Inc.	$330
1992	White-on-white quilt worked by Mary Ann Seeley, NY, 1833	Skinner, Inc.	$715
1992	Appliquéd and embroidered silk and cotton crazy quilt, American, 1902	Christie's NY	$110
1992	Embroidered cotton pictorial quilt, American, ca. 1930	Christie's NY	$2,090
1992	Watercolor, embroidered silk-and-velvet crazy quilt, initialed "H. N. C.," American, dated 1887	Christie's NY	$330
1992	Pieced and embroidered silk-and-velvet coverlet	Christie's NY	$330
1992	Amish pieced cotton-and-wool quilted and embroidered coverlet, IN, ca. 1930	Christie's NY	$1,540
1992	Pieced, appliquéd, and embroidered silk-and-velvet contained crazy quilt, American, ca. 1890	Christie's NY	$11,000
1992	Silk-and-velvet embroidered, pieced, and appliquéd contained crazy quilt, American, late 19th century	Christie's NY	$3,300
1992	Pieced and embroidered silk-and-velvet coverlet	Christie's NY	$275
1992	Amish pieced wool-and-cotton embroidered and quilted coverlet, Topeka, IN, dated 1899	Christie's NY	$7,700
1994	Crewel-embroidered linen bedcover attributed to Esther Meacham Strong, MA	Sotheby's NY	$9,200
1998	Crewel-embroidered cotton quilt, signed "Angeline Nowlen," dated May 23, 1864	Sotheby's NY	$9,200

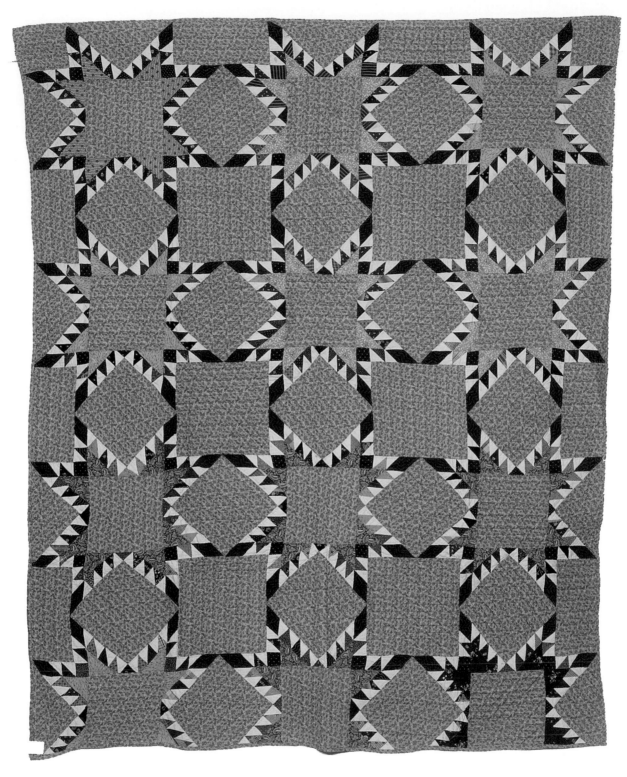

This Feathered Star quilt attributed to Lincoln, MO, circa 1860-1890, was sold in 2005 by Cowan's Auctions for $1,320. (Photograph courtesy of Cowan's Auctions, Inc.)

2004	Red on white quilt top, central block is of Pan American Exposition 1901, mounted and framed under glass, 6' x 6'	Winter Associates	$168
2005	White muslin with Diamond quilting, ca. 1940, 66" x 84"	Ken Farmer Auctions & Appraisals, LLC	$110
2005	Needlework wool; Paul family, South Solon, ME, ca. 1812–1814	James Julia	$97,750

Feathered Star

Year	Description	House	Price
1987	American appliquéd cotton Princess Feather pattern quilt, Hancock County, OH, ca. 1930	Butterfields	$770
1987	Fine Amish pieced cotton Star quilt, Lancaster County, PA, late 19th century	Butterfields	$3,850
1988	Blue-and-white jacquard woven coverlet, American, dated 1849	Butterfields	$412.50
1988	Two embroidered cotton quilts, American	Butterfields	$522.50
1990	Reversible Durham quilt	Christie's U.K.	£55
1991	Amish pieced cotton quilted coverlet, western PA or OH, ca. 1920	Christie's NY	$3,080
1991	Amish pieced wool quilted coverlet, Lancaster County, PA, ca. 1920	Christie's NY	$2,750
1991	Pieced quilt, American, late 19th/early 20th century	Skinner, Inc.	$330
1991	Amish quilted wool-and-wool crepe coverlet, probably Lancaster County, PA, ca. 1940	Christie's NY	$2,200
1991	Pieced quilt, American, late 19th/early 20th century	Skinner, Inc.	$715
1991	Pieced quilt, American, mid-19th century	Skinner, Inc.	$880
1991	Amish pieced cotton quilted coverlet, PA, ca. 1930	Christie's NY	$3,850
1991	Fine pieced and appliquéd cotton quilted coverlet attributed to Mary Brown, Calvert, MD, 1852	Christie's NY	$49,500
1991	Amish pieced wool-and-crepe quilted coverlet, Lancaster County, PA, ca. 1940	Christie's NY	$935
1991	Amish quilted wool coverlet initialed "A. S.," probably Lancaster County, PA, ca. 1925	Christie's NY	$2,640
1991	Pieced cotton quilted coverlet, American, 19th century	Christie's NY	$2,200
1991	Pieced and appliquéd cotton quilted coverlet, KS, mid-19th century	Christie's NY	$495
1991	Pieced cotton quilted coverlet, American, ca. 1890	Christie's NY	$770
1991	Pieced and appliquéd stuffed and quilted cotton coverlet, American, mid-19th century	Christie's NY	$2,200
1992	Amish pieced wool-and-cotton quilted coverlet, Lancaster, PA, ca. 1850	Christie's NY	$14,850
1998	Pieced and appliquéd cotton Feather Star quilt, 72" x 74"	Butterfields	$1,092.50
2005	Lincoln, MO area, ca. 1860-1890, 74" x 92"	Cowan's Auctions, Inc.	$1,320

During the 1999 sale of the Mr. and Mrs. James L. Britton collection, this meticulously quilted Floral pattern quilt was sold for $1,150. (Photograph courtesy of Christie's Images Ltd. 1999)

Floral Wreath

Year	Description	House	Price
1987	Extremely fine American appliquéd cotton and trapunto quilt, signed "Hannah Bervley, Joseph M. Thoreman," dated January 23, 1851	Butterfields	$4,125
1990	Pieced and quilted cotton coverlet, American, third quarter 19th century	Christie's NY	$528
1990	Pieced and appliquéd cotton quilted coverlet, American, late 19th/early 20th century	Christie's NY	$242
1990	White-on-white stuffed cotton quilt, signed and dated 1845	Christie's NY	$1,210
1991	Pieced cotton quilted coverlet, American, 19th century	Christie's NY	$2,200
1991	Amish pieced cotton quilted coverlet, probably Midwestern, ca. 1930	Christie's NY	$77
1991	White-on-white stuffed cotton quilted coverlet, American, early 19th century	Christie's NY	$2,200
1991	Pieced and appliquéd cotton quilted coverlet, PA, ca. 1850	Christie's NY	$3,850
1992	Pieced and appliquéd cotton quilted coverlet, American, ca. 1840	Christie's NY	$4,620
1992	Pieced and appliquéd cotton quilted coverlet, SC, mid-19th century	Christie's NY	$2,640
1992	Amish pieced wool-and-cotton quilted coverlet, Lancaster County, PA, ca. 1920	Christie's NY	$3,850
1994	Pieced and appliquéd cotton quilt, signed "Sarah Northrup, Lewisboro," dated March 1847	Sotheby's NY	$517
1994	Pieced calico-and-chintz quilt, 100" x 100"	Sotheby's NY	$546
1995	Fine pieced cotton quilt, Nancy Ogden Clearfield, Ferguson Township, PA, June 1878	Sotheby's NY	$1,840
1995	Three pieced cotton quilts, American	Sotheby's NY	$1,380
1998	Pieced and appliquéd cotton quilt, 88" x 76"	Sotheby's NY	$805
1999	American cotton quilt, 8' 5" x 6' 9"	Sloan's DC	$5,000
1999	Pieced and appliquéd cotton quilted coverlet	Christie's NY	$1,150
2001	Pieced and appliquéd Eagle and Flower cotton quilt, early 20th century	Butterfields	$1,880
2002	Appliquéd quilt, American, mid-19th century	Cowan's Auctions, Inc.	$747.50
2002	Early appliquéd quilt, signed "Vion Papin," ca. 1870	Cowan's Auctions, Inc.	$517.50
2002	Floral appliquéd quilt in Caesar's Crown pattern, American, mid-19th century	Cowan's Auctions, Inc.	$345
2003	Cotton floral chain, red border, heavy quilt stitching, provenance, mid-20th century, 80" x 89"	Thomaston Place Auction Galleries	$150
2003	White ground with sage green, red, and mustard colors, 85" x 85"	Ken Farmer Auctions & Appraisals, LLC	$1,200
2004	Vine and blackberry, 16 white blocks each with an appliquéd vine in aqua with pendant blackberries, ca. 1920, 82" x 86"	Skinner, Inc.	$3,995

2004	Flowers inside circles, vining leaf border, 87" x 87"	Alderfer Auction Company	$862.50
2004	Two quilts inscribed "Luraney P. Wheeler Jefferson Co. NY 1849," 8' 7" x 6' and 6' 11" x 7' 8"	Stair Galleries	$300
2004	Variation of the Rose Wreath pattern with 16 wreaths, mid-19th century	Skinner, Inc.	$470
2004	Sixteen white blocks separated by a diagonal red grid, New England, late 19th century, 80"½ x 90"	Skinner, Inc.	$1,410
2005	KY, Ca. 1860, 76" x 79"	Cowan's Auctions, Inc.	488.75
2005	CT, early 20th century, 86" x 76"	Pook & Pook, Inc.	$288
2005	Floral appliquéd quilt with stitched-in quilting, signed "Mary Ann Moore", mid-19th century, 98" x 92"	Alderfer Auction Company	$3,162.50
2005	Lancaster County, PA, 86" x 91"	Pook & Pook, Inc.	$1560
2005	Beaver Dam, KY area, mid-19th century, 81" square	Cowan's Auctions, Inc.	$2,760
2005	PA, late 19th century, 87" x 73"	Pook & Pook, Inc.	$374
2005	PA, late 19th century, 90" x 86"	Pook & Pook, Inc.	$2,040

Flower Basket

Year	Description	House	Price
1988	Two patchwork quilts, 20th century	Skinner, Inc.	$413
1990	Flower Basket patchwork and appliquéd quilt	Christie's U.K.	£418
1990	Flower Basket patchwork quilt	Christie's U.K.	£209
1990	Pieced and appliquéd quilt, American, second half 19th century	Skinner, Inc.	$990
1991	Pieced and appliquéd cotton quilted coverlet, Mary Swartz, Shiloh, OH, 1853	Christie's NY	$5,500
1991	Amish pieced cotton crib quilt, Midwestern, 1920-1940	Christie's NY	$990
1992	Quilt, 19th century, 86" x 86"	James Julia	$650
1992	Amish pieced wool-and-cotton quilted coverlet, Lancaster County, PA, ca. 1910	Christie's NY	$6,600
1992	Amish pieced wool-and-cotton quilted coverlet, Lancaster County, PA, ca. 1920	Christie's NY	$3,850
1992	Pieced and appliquéd cotton quilted coverlet, American, ca. 1930	Christie's NY	$88
1992	Amish cotton quilted coverlet, Midwestern, ca. 1930	Christie's NY	$1,045
1992	American appliquéd quilt with basket of flowers	Northeast Auctions	$375
1994	Copper-printed cotton quilt, signed "M. G. Ward"	Sotheby's NY	$546
1994	Pair of glazed chintz single-bed quilts, 54" x 64"	Sotheby's NY	$373
1995	Pieced calico quilt, ca. 1830	Sotheby's NY	$2,875
1995	Pieced and appliquéd calico-and-cotton Rose of Sharon quilt	Sotheby's NY	$690
1995	Pieced and appliquéd cotton Valley of Virginia quilt	Sotheby's NY	$1,380
1998	Appliquéd cotton Flower Basket quilt	Butterfields	$431.25
1998	Fine pieced red, yellow, and green Flower Basket quilt, 88" x 88"	Sotheby's NY	$2,300
1998	Pieced and appliquéd cotton quilt	Sotheby's NY	$1,150
1999	American cotton quilt, 6' 5" x 7' 7"	Sloan's DC	$550
2000	Fine handmade quilt flower pattern, 94" x 92"	James Julia	$143.75

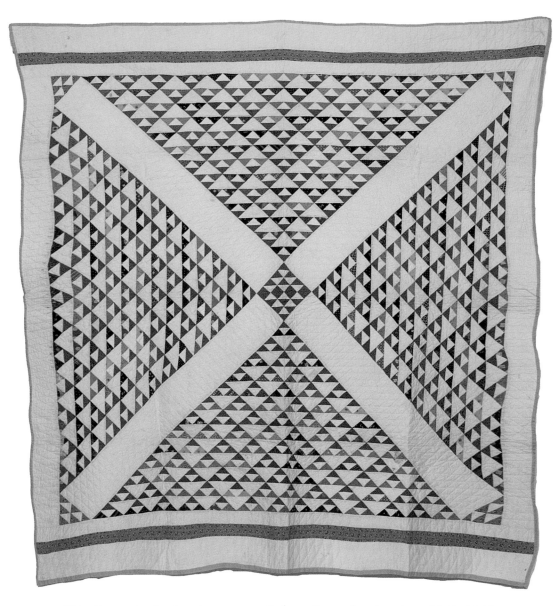

This Goose in the Pond pattern quilt from Pennsylvania, circa 1860-1880, was sold at a 2005 auction for $1,150. (Photograph courtesy of Cowan's Auctions, Inc.)

2001	Fabulous red, white, and blue needlepoint state-flower quilt, 83" x 90"	James Julia	$1,380
2001	Good appliquéd flower quilt, 72" x 84"	James Julia	$230
2003	Antique appliquéd flower quilt, 84" x 88"	James Julia	$230
2003	Signed in ink on one of the quilted flower pedals "Mary B. Raymond/at farm/1841," 86½" x 90"	Cowan's Auctions, Inc.	$747.50
2004	Baltimore Flower Basket pattern quilt, made by Elizabeth Livingston, Wilmington, PA, 1807, 84" x 86"	Skinner, Inc.	$9,987.50
2004	Yellow-and-white Basket quilt, possibly made by a Mennonite hand, ca. 1900, 79" x 79"	Skinner, Inc.	$1,527.50

| 2005 | Single Flower Basket square, 83" x 76" | Cowan's Auctions, Inc. | $805 |

Flyfoot

Year	Description	House	Price
1998	Pieced cotton Flyfoot quilt	Butterfields	$431.25
1998	Pieced cotton Flyfoot quilt, ca. 1900	Butterfields	$460
1998	Pieced cotton Flyfoot quilt, 63" x 77"	Butterfields	$431.25
1998	Amish pieced cotton Flyfoot quilt, Yoder family	Butterfields	$1,610

Flying Geese, Goose in the Pond

Year	Description	House	Price
1994	Pieced cotton Flying Geese crib quilt, New England, ca. 1860	Sotheby's NY	$1,955
1998	Pieced cotton Flying Geese quilt	Butterfields	$575
1999	Goose in the Pond patchwork quilt	Christie's U.K.	£460
2000	Brown and earth tone colors, late 19th century	Winter Associates	$220
2003	Bears label: Goshenhoppen Historians Quilt Roundup, 67" x 84"	Alderfer Auction Company	$632.50
2005	Triangle quilting, PA, ca. 1860–1880, 76" x 80"	Cowan's Auctions, Inc.	$1,150
2005	Early 20th century, 76" x 80"	Pook & Pook, Inc.	$316

Friendship

Year	Description	House	Price
1986	Rare Quaker friendship quilt	Robert Eldred Co.	$660
1988	Antique friendship quilt, American, dated 1886	Robert Eldred Co.	$413
1992	Nine Patch friendship quilt	Northeast Auctions	$650
1992	Pieced and appliquéd friendship quilt, SC, ca. 1850	Christie's NY	$4,400
1994	Pieced and appliquéd cotton friendship quilt, NJ, dated 1841	Sotheby's NY	$2,300
1998	Friendship quilt, 72" x 84"	Christie's U.K.	£253
2000	Framed, 19th century, 61" x 61"	Winter Associates	$1,210
2002	Friendship Star quilt, dated in one star March 6, 1847, 85" x 76"	James Julia	$316.25
2003	Each block is signed and dated with dates beginning in 1913 and extending through 1917, 58" x 76.5"	Cowan's Auctions, Inc.	$80.50
2004	Attached paper label, "given by Lucy Jackson Chaplin House," Bangor, ME, 1844	Skinner, Inc.	$470
2004	Friendship quilt, 5' 9" x 5' 5"	Thomaston Place Auction Galleries	$350
2004	Friendship quilt, ca. 1880–1890, 80" x 57"	Thomaston Place Auction Galleries	$225
2004	Friendship quilt, ca. 1880–1890, 80" x 57"	Thomaston Place Auction Galleries	$300
2004	Quilt, dated 1845, 104" x 105"	Pook & Pook, Inc.	$300
2004	Sixteen squares with red cotton calico appliquéd oak leaves, mid–19th century, 90" x 90"	Skinner, Inc.	$763.75
2005	Embroidered friendship quilt top by the van Houten, Blauvelt, Thomas families, and others, Rockland county, NY, dated 1860–1862, 88" x 86"	Sotheby's NY	$11,400
2005	NY, late 19th century, 84" x 93"	Pook & Pook, Inc.	$575

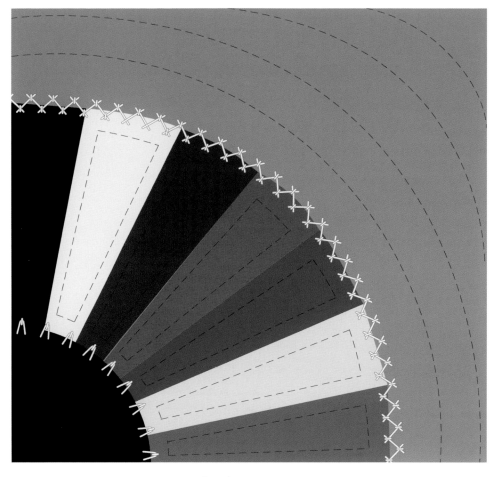

Grandmother's Fan pattern.

| 2005 | Pieced friendship quilt, late 19th century, 88" x 85" | Pook & Pook, Inc. | $460 |
| 2005 | Wilmington, VT, late 19th century, 86" x 90" | Pook & Pook, Inc. | $600 |

Grandmother's Fan

Year	Description	House	Price
1999	Pieced and appliquéd cotton quilted coverlet	Christie's NY	$1,035
2002	Paisley-backed pieced Log Cabin and Fan block pattern quilts	Skinner, Inc.	$206
2005	Decorative stitching on 24 fans, approx. 64" x 86"	Cowan's Auctions, Inc.	$201.25
2005	Strong jewel tones with embroidered accents, felt buttons, ruby and emerald borders, 81" x 66½"	Alderfer Auction Company	$161

Grandmother's Flower Garden

Year	Description	House	Price
1987	Rare Amish pieced wool-and-cotton crib quilt made by Mrs. C. B. (Lizzy) Miller, Chavin, Holmes County, OH	Butterfields	$2,475
1990	Grandmother's Flower Garden	Christie's U.K.	£286

1990	Grandmother's Flower Garden patchwork coverlet	Christie's U.K.	£27.50
1992	Pieced work quilt in Grandmother's Flower Garden pattern, 85½" x 69"	James Julia	$350
1996	American pieced silk quilt, ca. 1880	Sloan's DC	$600
1996	Pair pieced cotton quilts, American	Sloan's DC	$600
1998	Pieced cotton Flower Garden quilt, 76" x 80"	Butterfields	$1,035
1998	American Pillar pattern quilt, early 19th century	Sotheby's NY	$1,495
1998	Grandmother's Flower Garden quilt, 84" x 90"	Christie's U.K.	£207
1998	Grandmother's Flower Garden variation patchwork coverlet, 78" x 104"	Christie's U.K.	£149
1998	Shaped Grandmother's Flower Garden variation patchwork coverlet, 96" x 116"	Christie's U.K.	£253
1999	Grandmother's Flower Garden coverlet, 66" x 66"	Christie's U.K.	£161
1999	Grandmother's Flower Garden patchwork quilt, 110" x 98"	Christie's U.K.	£57
2001	Purple border, pastels, 98" x 83"	Winter Associates	$50.00
2002	Mosaic Diamonds quilt, American, ca. 1860s	Christie's U.K.	£199
2002	Multicolored from Nina Wilson Creel, who lived in the "Seven Mile House," Davisville, WV, 75" x 82"	Ken Farmer Auctions & Appraisals, LLC	$230
2004	Cotton quilt in multicolor pastels with scalloped border, early 1900s, 83" x 74½"	Ken Farmer Auctions & Appraisals, LLC	$275
2004	Pieced cotton Flower Garden quilt	Skinner, Inc.	$176.25
2005	Strawberry pink calico and green on white, ca. 1900, 72" x 100"	Cowan's Auctions, Inc.	$287.50
2005	Border interrupts the pattern, early 20th century, 73½" x 62"	Ken Farmer Auctions & Appraisals, LLC	$88

Hawaiian

Year	Description	House	Price
1991	Hawaiian appliquéd cotton quilted coverlet, ca. 1930	Christie's NY	$3,850
1991	Hawaiian pieced and appliquéd cotton quilted coverlet, ca. 1900	Christie's NY	$4,400
1998	Hawaiian pieced cotton counterpane	Butterfields	$345
1998	Appliquéd cotton Hawaiian quilt, 1925-1930	Sotheby's NY	$690
1999	Pieced and appliquéd cotton quilted coverlet	Christie's NY	$1,840
2005	Large red foliate medallion at center, 75" x 70"	Cowan's Auctions, Inc.	$862.50

Irish Chain

Year	Description	House	Price
1988	Two Irish Chain pattern quilts, American	Butterfields	$495
1990	Irish Chain variation quilt	Christie's U.K.	£253
1990	Irish Chain appliqué quilt, 80" square	Christie's U.K.	£143
1991	Amish pieced wool-and-crepe quilted coverlet, Lancaster County, PA, ca. 1940	Christie's NY	$935
1991	Appliquéd quilt, American, 19th century	Skinner, Inc.	$605

A Hawaiian quilt that sold in 2005 for $862.50. (Photograph courtesy of Cowan's Auctions, Inc.)

1991	Amish pieced quilt, probably Lancaster county, PA, late 19th/early 20th century	Skinner, Inc.	$1,540
1991	Pieced cotton quilted coverlet, American, 19th century	Christie's NY	$2,200
1992	Fine old Amish crib quilt, probably OH, ca. early 20th	James Julia	$550
1994	Amish pieced cotton Irish Chain crib quilt, OH, ca. 1825	Sotheby's NY	$920
1998	Pieced cotton double Irish Chain quilt, 78" x 70"	Butterfields	$920
1998	Pieced cotton double Irish Chain quilt	Butterfields	$1,495
1998	Double Irish Chain quilt	Christie's U.K.	£207
1998	Double Irish Chain quilt, 82" x 84"	Christie's U.K.	£299

1999	American cotton quilt, 5' 3" x 6' 9"	Sloan's DC	$140
1999	American cotton quilt, 7' 7" x 5' 10"	Sloan's DC	$600
1999	Amish pieced cotton-and-wool quilted coverlet, 80" x 76"	Christie's NY	$1,150
1999	Pieced cotton quilted coverlet	Christie's NY	$575
1999	Single Irish Chain quilt	Christie's U.K.	£207
2002	Red and blue on black, 82" x 67½"	Ken Farmer Auctions & Appraisals, LLC	$1,035
2003	Red, gold, and tan quilt, 19th century, 83" x 66"	Winter Associates	$84
2003	Double Irish Chain patchwork quilt, 84" x 71"	Alderfer Auction Company	$287.50
2003	Pieced and appliquéd quilted coverlet worked in orange fabric	Christie's NY	$598
2004	Double Irish Chain in pinks and green on white ground, 73" x 80"	Alderfer Auction Company	$172.50
2005	Red, white, and blue quilt, 19th century, 54" x 43"	Ken Farmer Auctions & Appraisals, LLC	$165.00
2005	Three Irish Chain quilts, ca. 1870, 83" x 87"	Pook & Pook, Inc.	$780
2005	NC, ca. 1900-1920, approx. 68" x 86"	Cowan's Auctions, Inc.	$204
2005	Triple Irish Chain pattern, late 19th century, 78" x 88"	Pook & Pook, Inc.	$316
2005	York County, PA, early 20th century, 71" x 83"	Pook & Pook, Inc.	$460

Jacob's Ladder

Year	Description	House	Price
2004	Pieced cotton Jacob's Ladder quilt	Skinner, Inc.	$352.50

Joseph's Coat

Year	Description	House	Price
1991	Pieced cotton quilted coverlet, eastern PA, ca. 1890	Christie's NY	$4,400
1992	Pieced cotton quilted coverlet, American, ca. 1880	Christie's NY	$880
1998	Pieced cotton Joseph's Coat quilt, mid–19th century	Sotheby's NY	$1,150
2004	Probably PA, approx. 80" x 84"	Sotheby's NY	$840

Log Cabin

Year	Description	House	Price
1987	Fine patchwork Log Cabin variant quilt, 75" x 66"	Robert Eldred Co.	$358
1987	Pieced Log Cabin pattern quilt, American, early 20th century	Butterfields	$357.50
1987	Pieced calico sampler quilt, PA, ca. 1920	Butterfields	$1,100
1988	Two American quilts	Butterfields	$495
1988	Group of four patchwork quilts	William Doyle Galleries	$660
1988	Two patchwork quilts, late 19th century	William Doyle Galleries	$330
1989	Appliquéd Log Cabin pattern child's quilt, 4' 4" x 5' 6"	Richard A. Bourne	$220
1989	Patchwork quilt, Log Cabin pattern, 88" x 78"	Robert Eldred Co.	$220
1990	Log Cabin patchwork coverlet, 80" x 68"	Christie's U.K.	£275
1990	Log Cabin patchwork coverlet	Christie's U.K.	£99
1990	Barn Raising, a Log Cabin variation patchwork coverlet	Christie's U.K.	£198

1990	Log Cabin variation patchwork quilt	Christie's U.K.	£143
1990	Log Cabin patchwork cover	Christie's U.K.	£165
1990	Log Cabin patchwork quilt	Christie's U.K.	£55
1990	Log Cabin patchwork coverlet	Christie's U.K.	£176
1991	Silk patchwork baby quilt, Log Cabin design, 38" x 52"	Robert Eldred Co.	$165
1991	Pieced quilt, American, second half 19th century	Skinner, Inc.	$330
1991	Three pieced quilts, American, third quarter 19th century	Skinner, Inc.	$605
1992	Pieced and appliquéd silk-and-cotton coverlet, American, ca. 1930	Christie's NY	$110
1992	Mennonite quilt in Log Cabin pattern, late 19th century, 72" x 72"	James Julia	$800
1992	Pieced cotton quilted coverlet, PA, ca. 1880	Christie's NY	$550
1994	Pieced cotton Log Cabin crib quilt, ca. 1899	Sotheby's NY	$1,495
1994	Two pieced calico Log Cabin quilts, 76" x 68"	Sotheby's NY	$1,265
1998	Barn Raising Log Cabin quilt	Christie's U.K.	£218
1998	Fine Barn Raising Log Cabin quilt	Christie's U.K.	£690
1998	Log Cabin coverlet, 62" x 72"	Christie's U.K.	£149
1998	Log Cabin Courthouse Steps variation patchwork quilt	Christie's U.K.	£322
1998	Pieced cotton Log Cabin child's quilt, American, late 19th century	Sotheby's NY	$805
1999	Log Cabin coverlet	Christie's U.K.	£138
1999	Pieced and wool reversible coverlet	Christie's NY	$345
1999	Pieced coverlet	Christie's NY	$58
2001	Multicolored calicoes, red center squares	Winter Associates	$110
2001	Multicolored solid and calico pieces	Winter Associates	$137.50
2001	Multicolored solid and calico pieces, blue-and-yellow floral	Winter Associates	$192.50
2002	Light and dark concentric squares, late 19th/early 20th century, 77" x 77"	Winter Associates	$412.50
2002	Paisley-backed pieced Log Cabin and Fan block pattern quilts	Skinner, Inc.	$206
2003	Courthouse Steps, 80" x 60"	Winter Associates	$39.20
2003	Early 20th century, 84" x 85"	Winter Associates	$476
2003	Log Cabin quilt, VT	Skinner, Inc.	$264.38
2003	Lot of two, Midwestern, both early 20th century, 76" x 81"; 71½" x 83"	Cowan's Auctions, Inc.	$86.25
2003	Pieced blocks in blue, brown, and green, 72" x 62"	Winter Associates	$89.60
2004	19th century, 73" x 75"	Winter Associates	$224
2004	Velvet and silk with maroon border, 19th century, 5' 7" x 4' 4"	Winter Associates	$224
2004	Backed in white cotton, 85" x 96"	Thomaston Place Auction Galleries	$275
2004	Bars in pastels and earth tones, brown-and-yellow bands at border, 77" x 87"	Alderfer Auction Company	$161
2004	Courthouse Steps with magenta centers, 79" x 77"	Winter Associates	$84
2005	Courthouse Steps in browns, reds, and greens, 89" x 79"	Alderfer Auction Company	$546.25
2005	Early 20th century, 92" x 76"	Pook & Pook, Inc.	$403
2005	Late 19th century, 77" x 84"	Pook & Pook, Inc.	$240

2005	Courthouse Step, dated in pencil on back, most in 1892, late 19th century, 38½" x 56"	Winter Associates	$224
2005	New England, ca. 1900, 86" x 77"	Pook & Pook, Inc.	$374
2005	NY, early 20th century, 76" x 84"	Pook & Pook, Inc.	$345
2005	PA, late 19th century, 57" x 57"	Pook & Pook, Inc.	$115

Lone Eagle

Year	Description	House	Price
1998	Pieced cotton Lindbergh Lone Eagle quilt, 73" x 74"	Butterfields	$747.50
2003	Four rows of five images of the *Spirit of St. Louis*, ca. 1927, 70" x 84"	Cowan's Auctions, Inc.	$862.50

Lone Star, Star of Bethlehem, Mennonite Star, Evening Star, Star

Year	Description	House	Price
1989	Appliquéd quilt, Lone Star pattern	Richard A. Bourne	$220
1991	Pieced cotton quilted coverlet, American, ca. 1890	Christie's NY	$770
1994	Fine pieced and appliquéd cotton-and-chintz Star of Bethlehem quilt, NY, ca. 1825	Sotheby's NY	$5,750
1994	Pieced and cotton Mennonite Star quilt, 86" x 78"	Sotheby's NY	$2,300
1995	Fine pieced cotton album quilt, ca. 1850	Sotheby's NY	$1,265
1995	Pieced calico-and-cotton Star quilt	Sotheby's NY	$632
1995	Rare linsey-woolsey quilt, New England, 1780-1790	Sotheby's NY	$2,300
1996	Pieced cotton quilt, American	Sloan's DC	$525
1996	Pieced silk quilt, American	Sloan's DC	$3,000
1998	Pieced sateen-and-cotton Broken Star quilt, signed "M. R.," 1918	Butterfields	$1,495
1998	Pieced and appliquéd cotton trapunto Star and Rose quilt, 91" x 91"	Butterfields	$1,035
1998	Pieced cotton Broken Star quilt, Holmes County, OH	Butterfields	$1,610
1998	Evening Star patchwork quilt, 72" x 88"	Christie's U.K.	£184
1998	Pieced cotton Star of Bethlehem quilt	Sotheby's NY	$2,300
1998	Star of Bethlehem Broken Star variation quilt, 88" x 86"	Christie's U.K.	£483
1998	Two pieced cotton Star of Bethlehem quilts	Sotheby's NY	$1,380
1999	Cotton quilt, American, 6' 3" x 6' 6"	Sloan's DC	$175
1999	Pair of pieced and appliquéd cotton quilted pillow cases	Christie's NY	$1,725
1999	Pieced and appliquéd cotton quilted coverlet	Christie's NY	$575
1999	Pieced and appliquéd cotton quilted coverlet, 75" x 72"	Christie's NY	$690
1999	Pieced and appliquéd cotton quilted coverlet, 94" x 93"	Christie's NY	$575
1999	Star quilt, 80" x 80"	Christie's U.K.	£230
2001	Large Star patchwork quilt, 72" x 82"	James Julia	$201.25
2002	Yellow, brown, and cream, 20th century, 100" x 84"	Winter Associates	$165
2002	Eight-pointed pieced Star quilt, American, late 19th/early 20th century	Cowan's Auctions, Inc.	$258.75

Attributed as a circa-1870-1890 Pennsylvania Broken Star quilt, it sold for $1,150 at a 2004 Cowan's Auction sale. (Photograph courtesy of Cowan's Auctions, Inc.)

2002	Red, white, and blue with red-and-blue borders from Nina Wilson Creel, who lived in the "Seven Mile House," Davisville, WV, 77" x 80"	Ken Farmer Auctions & Appraisals, LLC	$287.50
2003	Sixteen eight-pointed stars pieced in yellow, red, and green calico, 103" x 100"	Alderfer Auction Company	$1,725
2003	Composed of nine eight-pointed stars enclosed in a swag and tassel border, 19th century, 103" x 103"	Skinner, Inc.	$2,585
2003	Composed of 16 eight-pointed stars arranged in a grid, 19th century, 82" x 83"	Skinner, Inc.	$705

Star of Bethlehem pattern.

2003	Red and yellow, 19th century, 74" x 96"	Cowan's Auctions, Inc.	$195.50
2003	Central polychrome eight-pointed star, with smaller eight-pointed stars in field, 81" x 81"	Alderfer Auction Company	$690
2003	Blue, red, green, and pink, late 19th century or later	Ken Farmer Auctions & Appraisals, LLC	$350
2003	White background with multicolored stars, 81" x 69"	Ken Farmer Auctions & Appraisals, LLC	$130
2003	Red and white	Winter Associates	$84
2003	Signed and dated on back "Edith W. Smith 1931," 8' x 6' 2"	Winter Associates	$392
2004	Made by "William Ann Norville 1823-1911 Temperance Hall North Carolina," ca. 1840-60, 7' 6" x 8' 6"	Thomaston Place Auction Galleries	$4,500

Attributed to Clarksville, TN, circa 1860, this Star quilt was sold by Cowan's Auctions in 2004 for $1,265. (Photograph courtesy of Cowan's Auctions, Inc.)

2004	Forty-two blocks of eight-pointed stars, ca. 1870, 80" x 90"	Skinner, Inc.	$1,762.50
2004	Twelve multipointed stars and vining floral border, ca. 1870-1880, 78" x 96"	Cowan's Auctions, Inc.	$1,265
2004	Eight-pointed green-and-pink calico stars on a white calico ground, 72" x 80"	Alderfer Auction Company	$161
2004	Large eight-pointed star in pastel colors, quilting in star motif in white areas, 69" square	Alderfer Auction Company	$80.50

2004	Quilt with 156 stars in brown, red, green, and blue, late 19th/early 20th century, 75" x 80"	Winter Associates	$140
2004	Multiple eight-pointed polychrome calico stars, 87" x 59"	Alderfer Auction Company	$57.50
2004	One eight-pointed star with tulips between the points, 83" x 84"	Alderfer Auction Company	$2,875
2004	One large eight-pointed star formed from red, green, and yellow calicos, 72" x 72"	Alderfer Auction Company	$460
2004	Star of Bethlehem pattern, 67" x 62"	Winter Associates	$140
2004	Star of the East quilt, probably PA, 19th century, approx. 100" x 92"	Sotheby's NY	$1,080
2005	Alternating green blocks and green border strip, 19th century, 79" x 84"	Winter Associates	$28
2005	Large central star flanked by four smaller stars and four partial stars, ca. 1920-1930, approx. 82" square	Cowan's Auctions, Inc.	$402.50
2005	Columbus, OH, ca. 1930, 64" x 66"	Pook & Pook, Inc.	$316
2005	Early 20th century, 94" x 86"	Pook & Pook, Inc.	$360
2005	Nine stars, late 19th century, 86" x 87"	Pook & Pook, Inc.	$489
2005	Radiant stars, polychrome cottons, 91" x 90"	Alderfer Auction Company	$805
2005	Wayne County, OH, ca. 1940, 82" x 76"	Pook & Pook, Inc.	$510

Mariner's Compass

Year	Description	House	Price
1988	Mariner's Compass quilt, 6' 6" x 5' 6"	Grogan & Co.	$300
1991	Pieced and appliquéd cotton quilted coverlet, American, late 19th century	Christie's NY	$770
1991	Pieced and appliquéd quilt, American, late 19th century	Skinner, Inc.	$825
1991	Pieced and appliquéd quilted cotton coverlet, American, mid-19th century	Christie's NY	$2,420
1991	Pieced and appliquéd stuffed and quilted cotton coverlet, American, mid-19th century	Christie's NY	$2,200
1995	Three pieced cotton quilts, American	Sotheby's NY	$1,380
1998	Pieced cotton Mariner's Compass quilt	Butterfields	$1,150
1998	Pieced and appliquéd Mariner's Compass quilt	Butterfields	$517.50
2000	Early Mariner's Compass quilt, 82" x 78"	James Julia	$862.50
2001	Pieced and appliquéd cotton Mariner's Compass quilt, ca. 1880	Butterfields	$881.25
2002	Blue and brown on white with red border, ca. 1850, 85" x 70"	Winter Associates	$357.50
2003	Pieced and appliquéd quilted coverlet centering a Compass Star	Christie's NY	$2,868
2005	Attributed to Shelbyville, TN, ca 1840-1850, approx. 80" x 90"	Cowan's Auctions, Inc.	$2,300

Medallion

Year	Description	House	Price
1987	Extremely fine appliquéd cotton and trapunto quilt, signed "Hannah Bervley, Joseph M. Thoreman," American, dated January 23, 1851	Butterfields	$4,125

This Mariner's Compass pattern quilt from Shelbyville, TN, circa 1840-1850, was sold in 2005 for $2,300. (Photograph courtesy of Cowan's Auctions, Inc.)

1987	Pieced calico-and-cotton quilt, American, late 19th/early 20th century	Butterfields	$770
1988	Blue-and-white jacquard woven coverlet, American, dated 1849	Butterfields	$412.50
1989	Appliqué quilt, York County, PA, ca. 1865	Skinner, Inc.	$1,320
1989	Appliquéd floral quilt, American, last half of 19th century	Skinner, Inc.	$385
1990	Appliquéd quilt, American, 19th century	Skinner, Inc.	$825
1990	Linsey-woolsey quilted coverlet, early 19th century	Christie's NY	$2,640
1990	Silk quilt, France, late 18th/early 19th century	Skinner, Inc.	$3,575
1990	Durham quilt of peach-colored sateen	Christie's U.K.	£121
1990	Durham quilt of pale yellow sateen, 76" x 90"	Christie's U.K.	£308
1990	Yellow quilt	Christie's U.K.	£60.50

1990	Reversible Durham quilt of pale pink sateen	Christie's U.K.	£99
1990	Durham quilt of olive green sateen	Christie's U.K.	£198
1990	Pink Durham quilt, reversing to green	Christie's U.K.	£77
1990	Reversible Durham quilt of white sateen	Christie's U.K.	£165
1990	Durham quilt of pink sateen	Christie's U.K.	£99
1990	Green Durham quilt, reversing to primrose yellow	Christie's U.K.	£88
1990	Marcella quilt with a central medallion	Christie's U.K.	£121
1990	Reversible Durham quilt of white sateen, 92" x 80"	Christie's U.K.	£165
1990	Cream-colored Durham quilt, reversing to pale pink	Christie's U.K.	£154
1990	Amish pieced cotton-and-wool quilted coverlet, Lancaster County, PA	Christie's NY	$1,540
1990	White-on-white stuffed cotton quilt, signed and dated 1845	Christie's NY	$1,210
1991	Pieced and appliquéd cotton quilted coverlet, Mary Swartz, Shiloh, OH, 1853	Christie's NY	$5,500
1991	Pieced cotton quilted coverlet, American, late 19th century	Christie's NY	$1,430
1991	Pieced and appliquéd quilted cotton coverlet, American, mid-19th century	Christie's NY	$4,400
1991	Amish pieced cotton quilted coverlet, Lancaster County, PA, ca. 1930	Christie's NY	$880
1991	Hawaiian pieced and appliquéd cotton quilted coverlet, 20th century	Christie's NY	$1,100
1991	White-on-white stuffed cotton quilted coverlet, American, early 19th century	Christie's NY	$2,200
1991	Pieced cotton quilted coverlet, American, late 19th century	Christie's NY	$1,430
1991	White-on-white corded cotton crib quilt, probably American, 1790-1810	Christie's NY	$1,870
1991	White-on-white stuffed cotton quilt stenciled "Eunice H. Stratton Wendell," American, 1836	Christie's NY	$4,620
1991	Amish pieced cotton quilted coverlet, Lancaster County, PA, ca. 1930	Christie's NY	$880
1991	Hawaiian pieced and appliquéd cotton quilted coverlet, 20th century, 80" x 90"	Christie's NY	$1,100
1991	White-on-white stuffed cotton crib quilt, probably American, 1790-1810	Christie's NY	$2,640
1991	Pieced and appliquéd quilt, American, 20th century	Skinner, Inc.	$550
1991	Pieced cotton quilted coverlet, American, late 19th century, 88" x 88"	Christie's NY	$1,430
1992	Pieced and appliquéd cotton quilted sampler coverlet, American, ca. 1880	Christie's NY	$880
1992	Pieced and appliquéd cotton quilted coverlet, SC, ca. 1830	Christie's NY	$4,400
1992	Pieced and appliquéd cotton quilted coverlet, American, ca. 1880	Christie's NY	$3,080
1992	Pair of double-woven dark and light blue jacquard coverlets attributed to David Harring, Bergen County, NJ, 1838	Christie's NY	$2,200

| 1992 | Pieced and appliquéd quilted cotton coverlet | Christie's NY | $715 |

Nine Patch

Year	Description	House	Price
1991	An Amish pieced cotton crib quilt, Midwestern, ca. 1910	Christie's NY	$2,860
1991	Antique Amish patchwork Nine Patch pattern quilt, PA, 84" x 66"	Sloan's DC	$190
1992	Amish pieced wool-and-cotton quilted coverlet, Lancaster County, PA, ca. 1925	Christie's NY	$3,520
1992	Nine Patch friendship quilt in red, yellow, and green	Northeast Auctions	$650
1998	Pieced cotton Nine Patch Star quilt	Butterfields	$488.75
1998	Pieced cotton Nine Patch quilt	Butterfields	$1,265
1998	Nine Patch quilt, dated 1882, 64" x 72"	Christie's U.K.	£920
2000	Three quilts, late 19th/early 20th century	Winter Associates	$55
2002	Double Nine Patch pattern pieced quilt, American, mid-19th century	Cowan's Auctions, Inc.	$373.75
2002	Large appliquéd red-and-white quilt, 98" x 98"	James Julia	$115
2002	Multicolored quilt from Nina Wilson Creel, who lived in the "Seven Mile House," Davisville, WV, 61" x 80"	Ken Farmer Auctions & Appraisals, LLC	$258.75
2002	Pink and blue on a green field with a black border, 73" x 64"	Ken Farmer Auctions & Appraisals, LLC	$862.50
2002	Quilt with violet border from Nina Wilson Creel, who lived in the "Seven Mile House," Davisville, WV, 66" x 81"	Ken Farmer Auctions & Appraisals, LLC	$230
2003	Peach, cream, and black, ca. 1920, 87" x 70"	Ken Farmer Auctions & Appraisals, LLC	$300
2005	Blue and white with blue inner border and binding, ca. 1900, 80" x 79"	Ken Farmer Auctions & Appraisals, LLC	$192.50
2005	PA, ca. 1910, 84" x 98"	Pook & Pook, Inc.	$690
2005	Triple border in red and black-and-white calico, plain linen backing, 79" x 81"	Cowan's Auctions, Inc.	$345.00
2005	Turkey tracks, PA, ca. 1870, 90" x 90"	Pook & Pook, Inc.	$431

New York Beauty

Year	Description	House	Price
1991	Pieced and appliquéd cotton quilted coverlet, American, ca. 1870	Christie's NY	$605
1991	Pieced and appliquéd cotton quilted coverlet, American, late 19th century	Christie's NY	$880
1991	Pieced cotton quilted coverlet, American, late 19th century	Christie's NY	$1,430
1992	Appliquéd and stuffed cotton quilt, MD, ca. 1825	Christie's NY	$1,210

Ocean Waves

Year	Description	House	Price
1987	American pieced calico Ocean Waves pattern quilt, MO, early 20th century	Butterfields	$467.50
1998	Pieced and cotton Ocean Waves quilt	Butterfields	$2,587.50
1998	Pieced cotton Ocean Waves quilt, 86" x 78"	Butterfields	$862.50
1998	Pieced cotton Ocean Waves quilt	Butterfields	$1,035
1999	Cotton quilt, American, 82" x 70"	Sloan's DC	$150
2002	Multicolored on a green background, tan inner border and green outer border, 80" x 70"	Ken Farmer Auctions & Appraisals, LLC	$1,380

Patriotic

Year	Description	House	Price
1990	Pieced and appliquéd quilt, American, late 19th/early 20th century	Skinner, Inc.	$935
1991	Pieced and appliquéd cotton quilted coverlet, PA, 1910	Christie's NY	$935
1992	Pieced and appliquéd cotton album quilt top, New England, ca. 1850	Christie's NY	$2,860
1998	Printed felt Flag quilt, 56" x 66"	Butterfields	$230
1998	Printed silk Flag quilt, 51" x 52"	Butterfields	$2,300
1998	Eagle appliquéd quilt, 80" x 96"	Christie's U.K.	£920
1999	Commemorative American cotton quilt, 7' 8" x 6' 6"	Sloan's DC	$600
1999	Fine pieced and appliquéd cotton Victory quilt, signed "Mrs. W. B. Lathouse," Warren, OH, ca. 1945	Sotheby's NY	$4,887
1999	Pieced and appliquéd cotton Century of Progress quilt, ca. 1945	Sotheby's NY	$5,462
1999	Pieced and appliquéd cotton quilted coverlet	Christie's NY	$230
1999	Pieced and appliquéd red, white, and blue cotton American Flag quilt, ca. 1900	Sotheby's NY	$12,650
1999	Pieced and appliquéd red, white, and blue cotton American Flag with central medallion Civil War quilt, ca. 1865	Sotheby's NY	$12,650
1999	Pieced and appliquéd red, white, and blue Union quilt, ca. 1915	Sotheby's NY	$8,050
1999	Pieced cotton Centennial quilt, probably PA, dated 1876	Sotheby's NY	$6,325
1999	Pieced cotton crib quilt	Christie's NY	$460
1999	Pieced red, white, and blue cotton American Flag quilt, probably PA, late 19th/early 20th century	Sotheby's NY	$2,185
1999	Unusual pieced and appliquéd printed cotton Kerchief quilt, ca. 1876	Sotheby's NY	$9,200
1999	Unusual pieced and appliquéd red, white, and blue concentric Bars and Stars quilt, ca. 1915	Sotheby's NY	$7,475
2000	Flag quilt, American, ca. 1930, 72" x 85"	Sotheby's NY	$5,700
2002	Fabulous red, white, and blue needlepoint state-flower quilt, 83" x 90"	James Julia	$1,380

2002	Pieced and appliquéd cotton Union quilt, probably PA, ca. 1915	Skinner Inc.	$9,988
2003	Red, white, and blue Patriotic Stars, nine rows, 94" x 88"	Ken Farmer Auctions & Appraisals, LLC	$250
2004	Appliqued calico cotton on a white muslin, banner with stitched lettering *"E PLURIBUS UNUM"* over "WASHINGTON" on horseback and "LIBERTY," Signed "C.C. SHUFELT 1853," 77" x 97"	Skinner, Inc.	$8,225
2004	Eagle quilt, 19th or 20th century	Skinner, Inc.	$763.75
2004	Eagles and Sunburst quilt with a central teal and red sunburst surrounded by four teal and red eagles and shields, 76" x 81"	Alderfer Auction Company	$1,380
2004	Patchwork quilt of corduroy stitched in a Star pattern, 65" x 61"	Alderfer Auction Company	$34.50
2005	Eagle quilt, Union county, PA, ca. 1870-1880, approx. 80" x 85"	Sotheby's NY	$5,400
2005	Eagle appliquéd and strawberry-border quilt, probably PA, ca. 1870-1880, 84" x 86"	Sotheby's NY	$1,080

Pictorial

Year	Description	House	Price
1990	Album quilt, American, mid-19th century	Skinner, Inc.	$3,080
1991	Fine pieced and appliquéd cotton quilted coverlet attributed to Mary Brown, Calvert, MD, 1852	Christie's NY	$49,500
1991	Rare Amish cotton quilted coverlet, Lancaster County, PA, ca. 1920	Christie's NY	$5,500
1991	Tied quilt, American, late 19th century	Skinner, Inc.	$550
1992	Embroidered cotton pictorial quilt, American, ca. 1930	Christie's NY	$2,090
1992	Pieced and appliquéd crazy quilt, American, ca. 1930	Christie's NY	$715
1995	Unusual pieced, appliquéd, and reverse-appliquéd cotton quilt, dated 1852	Sotheby's NY	$1,610
1995	Unusual pieced cotton quilt, ca. 1930	Sotheby's NY	$632
2001	Birds of the United States, 20th century, 84" x 90"	Winter Associates	$125
2002	New England village scene quilt, 20th century, 84" x 86"	Winter Associates	$110
2003	Magenta pennant with the name "MARY EDSON," a blue flag with thirty stars, and a white flag with embroidered numbers "8215," made by Hope Atkins Howes, American, third quarter 19th century, 72" x 90"	Skinner, Inc.	$1,527.50
2004	Outstanding commemorative quilt with airships, Akron, OH, approx. 85" x 65"	Cowan's Auctions, Inc.	$3,450
2004	Silk panels with animals, fruit, Indian tobacco, and religious phrases, 53¼" x 52"	Winter Associates	$252
2004	Trapunto and embroidered pictorial quilt: the homestead, signed "F. Cochran," probably KS, ca. 1910, approx. 72" x 92"	Sotheby's NY	$48,000

This American pictorial quilt was attributed to Hope Atkins Howes, third quarter 19th century, and sold in 2003 for $1527.50. A note written by a descendant of the maker accompanied the quilt. It read, "Captain Daniel H Howes died in Philadelphia of yellow fever on May 19th, 1879 at age 49-three months. On the deck of the Mary Edson is his wife Hopie Atkins Howes and son Daniel Howes on a trip to China. On this trip his wife made this quilt. Captain Howes is buried in the Union Cemetery in Chatham, Mass." (Photograph courtesy of Skinner, Inc. Bolton, MA)

During an important American sale on January 24 through 30, 1995, Sotheby's placed one of America's purportedly highest-priced quilts on the auction block. The provenance was attributed to Eileen Mackey Hackman of Perkinsville, Pennsylvania, and Middleburg, Virginia. Dated late-nineteenth-century vintage, this quilt was estimated at $20,000 to $30,000—an unheard-of price for a 1995-era quilt sale. No winning bid was realized for this quilt, however.

Pine Tree

Year	Description	House	Price
1987	Pieced calico-and-cotton Pine Tree pattern quilt, American, late 19th century	Butterfields	$247.50
1996	American coverlet, 44" x 90"	Sloan's DC	$450

Pinwheel

Year	Description	House	Price
1987	American pieced cotton Monkey Wrench pattern quilt, MO, 1930	Butterfields	$660

1987	American pieced calico and cotton quilt, late 19th/early 20th century	Butterfields	$770
1988	Pieced album quilt, American, ca 1851–1886	Skinner, Inc.	$413
1990	Patchwork quilt	Christie's U.K.	£176
1991	Hand-sewn quilt, 75" x 83"	Robert Eldred Co.	$220
1992	Pieced and appliquéd cotton quilted coverlet, American, early 20th century	Christie's NY	$2,970
1992	Linsey-woolsey quilted coverlet, American, late 18th century	Christie's NY	$3,850
1992	Rare Amish or Mennonite pieced cotton quilted coverlet, Martin M. Lichty, Lancaster County, PA, 1879	Christie's NY	$6,050
1992	Amish pieced wool-and-cotton quilted coverlet, Lancaster County, PA, ca. 1920	Christie's NY	$3,850
1992	Pair of double-woven dark and light blue jacquard coverlets attributed to David Harring, Bergen County, NJ, 1838	Christie's NY	$2,200
1998	Pieced cotton Pinwheel quilt	Butterfields	$862.50
1999	American cotton quilt, 6' 9" x 6' 6"	Sloan's DC	$200
1999	Pinwheel quilt, 80" x 100"	Christie's U.K.	£207
2002	Lot of five, includes four pinwheel quilt patterns, 19th century, 4½" to 17" in diameter	Cowan's Auctions, Inc.	$373.75
2004	19th century	Winter Associates	$224
2005	Ca. 1930, 78" x 78"	Pook & Pook, Inc.	$403

Postage Stamp

Year	Description	House	Price
1998	Pieced cotton Postage Stamp quilt, 72" x 81"	Butterfields	$805
1998	Pieced cotton Postage Stamp quilt, dated 1933	Butterfields	$747.50
1998	Pieced cotton Postage Stamp quilt, 65" x 76"	Butterfields	$1,150
1998	Pieced cotton Postage Stamp quilt	Butterfields	$1,840
2005	IN, ca. 1930, approx. 84" x 89"	Cowan's Auctions, Inc.	$488.75
2005	Pieced crib quilt, PA, early 20th century, 42" x 35"	Pook & Pook, Inc.	$403

Princess Feather

Year	Description	House	Price
1986	Appliquéd quilt	Robert Eldred Co.	$385
1987	American appliquéd cotton Princess Feather pattern quilt, Hancock County, OH, ca. 1930	Butterfields	$770
1988	American blue-and-white jacquard woven coverlet, dated 1849	Butterfields	$412.50
1990	Pieced and appliquéd cotton quilted coverlet, probably NJ	Christie's NY	$2,860
1991	Amish pieced wool-and-crepe quilted coverlet, Lancaster County, PA, ca. 1940	Christie's NY	$935
1991	Amish pieced cotton quilted coverlet, PA, ca. 1930	Christie's NY	$3,850
1991	Amish pieced cotton quilted coverlet, western PA or OH, ca. 1920	Christie's NY	$3,080

A richly detailed Princess Feather quilt in a Basket pattern.

1991	Pieced and appliquéd cotton quilted coverlet, KS, mid-19th century	Christie's NY	$495
1991	Pieced cotton quilted coverlet, American, 19th century	Christie's NY	$2,200
1991	Appliquéd cotton quilted coverlet, OH, ca. 1850	Christie's NY	$2,420
1991	Pieced and appliquéd cotton quilted coverlet, PA, ca. 1850	Christie's NY	$3,850
1991	Amish pieced wool quilted coverlet, Lancaster County, PA, ca. 1920	Christie's NY	$2,750
1991	Amish pieced cotton-and-wool quilted coverlet, probably Holmes County, OH, 1908	Christie's NY	$4,400
1991	Amish pieced wool quilted coverlet, Lancaster County, PA, ca. 1920	Christie's NY	$2,200
1991	Pieced cotton quilted coverlet, American, ca. 1890	Christie's NY	$770
1991	White-on-white stuffed and quilted cotton coverlet, American, dated 1810	Christie's NY	$3,850
1991	Amish pieced and appliquéd quilted cotton coverlet, probably OH, ca. 1920	Christie's NY	$1,650
1991	Pieced and appliquéd stuffed and quilted cotton coverlet, American, mid-19th century	Christie's NY	$2,200
1991	Pieced and appliquéd quilted cotton coverlet, American, mid-19th century	Christie's NY	$2,420
1991	Amish quilted wool-and-wool crepe coverlet, probably Lancaster County, PA, ca. 1940	Christie's NY	$2,200
1992	Amish pieced wool-and-cotton quilted coverlet Lancaster County, PA, ca. 1925	Christie's NY	$3,520
1992	Blue linsey-woolsey quilted coverlet, American, early 19th century	Christie's NY	$4,950
1992	Pieced and appliquéd quilted cotton crib coverlet, OH, 19th century	Christie's NY	$220
1992	Amish pieced wool-and-cotton embroidered and quilted coverlet, Topeka, IN, dated 1899	Christie's NY	$7,700
1992	Pieced and appliquéd cotton quilted coverlet, probably Dover, OH, ca. 1875	Christie's NY	$1,540
1992	Red linsey-woolsey quilted coverlet, American, early 19th century	Christie's NY	$2,090
1992	Pieced and appliquéd cotton quilted coverlet, American, ca. 1880	Christie's NY	$3,080
1992	Amish pieced wool-and-cotton quilted coverlet, Lancaster County, PA, ca. 1930	Christie's NY	$1,650
1992	Amish pieced wool-and-cotton quilted coverlet, Lancaster County, PA, ca. 1850	Christie's NY	$14,850
1998	Pieced cotton Princess Feather quilt	Butterfields	$1,035
1998	Pieced and appliquéd cotton quilt, 78" x 68"	Sotheby's NY	$1,150
1999	Amish pieced and appliquéd cotton-and-wool quilted coverlet	Christie's NY	$1,995
1999	Pieced and appliquéd cotton quilted coverlet, 82" x 79"	Christie's NY	$920
2004	American, 19th century, approx. 88" x 80"	Sotheby's NY	$2,040

| 2004 | Hand-pieced and quilted in Princess Feather design in solid red, green, and yellow ocher cotton fabrics, ca. 1900-1910, 80" x 94" | Cowan's Auctions, Inc. | $690 |

Rail Fence

Year	Description	House	Price
1996	Amish pieced cotton quilt, OH, March 1933, 67" x 76"	Sloan's DC	$1,100

Robbing Peter to Pay Paul

Year	Description	House	Price
1998	Pieced cotton Robbing Peter to Pay Paul variant quilt and pillow cover	Butterfields	$517.50
1999	Pieced cotton quilted coverlet, 94" x 83"	Christie's NY	$235
1999	Pieced cotton quilted coverlet	Christie's NY	$805
1999	Rare and unusual pieced and stuffed cotton Turtle quilt, southern, probably GA	Sotheby's NY	$12,650

Sampler

Year	Description	House	Price
1987	American pieced and appliquéd cotton sampler quilt, late 19th/early 20th century	Butterfields	$1,210
1987	American pieced calico sampler quilt, PA, ca. 1920	Butterfields	$1,100
1987	American appliquéd cotton sampler quilt, inscribed "Cora Erwin," ca. 1920	Butterfields	$467.50
1990	Sampler	Christie's U.K.	£2,750
1990	Sampler by Caroline Partridge, 1839	Christie's U.K.	£330
1990	Sampler with the inscription "Sarah Butler her piece Plymtree school 1796"	Christie's U.K.	£242
1990	Sampler by Sarah Eawoods, 1794	Christie's U.K.	£220
1990	Long sampler	Christie's U.K.	£1,430
1990	Sampler by Ann Bampton, 1797	Christie's U.K.	£143
1990	Sampler by Ellen Barnett	Christie's U.K.	£308
1992	Floral sampler pattern quilt within a grid	Northeast Auctions	$175
1992	Pieced and appliquéd cotton quilted sampler coverlet, American, ca. 1880	Christie's NY	$880
1998	Pieced and appliquéd cotton sampler variant quilt	Butterfields	$546.25
1998	Pieced cotton sampler quilt	Butterfields	$575

Schoolhouse

Year	Description	House	Price
1987	American pieced cotton Schoolhouse pattern quilt, late 19th century	Butterfields	$715
1991	Pieced calico Schoolhouse quilt, Albuquerque,		

	NM, ca. 1930, 84" x 61"	Sotheby's NY	$1,800
1992	Pieced and appliquéd cotton quilted coverlet, American, early 20th century	Christie's NY	$2,970
1995	American pieced and appliquéd cotton Schoolhouse quilt	Sotheby's NY	$575
1998	Pieced cotton Schoolhouse quilt, 73" x 80"	Butterfields	$977.50
1999	Pieced and appliquéd cotton quilted coverlet	Christie's NY	$345
2003	Composed of 16 red Schoolhouse designs on a white field, 19th century, 74" x 77"	Skinner, Inc.	$411.25

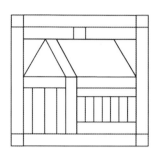

The piecework for the Schoolhouse pattern.

Schoolhouse pattern.

Snail's Trail

Year	Description	House	Price
1999	Pieced and appliquéd cotton quilted coverlet	Christie's NY	$1,150

Spinning Top

Year	Description	House	Price
1998	Pieced cotton Spinning Top quilt	Butterfields	$1,725

Strip

Year	Description	House	Price
1989	Child's cotton quilt and four boxed paper toys, late 18th/early 19th century	Skinner, Inc.	$715
1990	Durham quilt of primrose-yellow sateen, 76" x 84"	Christie's U.K.	£154
1990	Reversible Durham quilt of gold-colored sateen	Christie's U.K.	£27.50
1990	Strip quilt	Christie's U.K.	£110
1990	Strip quilt, early 19th century	Skinner, Inc.	$423

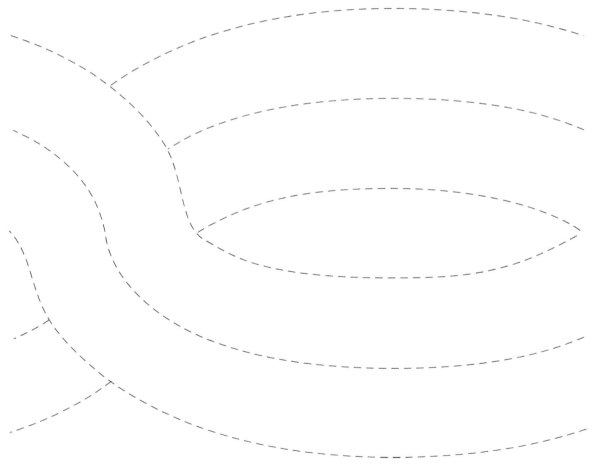

Snail's Trail pattern.

1990	Patchwork quilt	Christie's U.K.	£66
1990	Strip quilt composed of primrose-yellow and white sateen	Christie's U.K.	£198
1990	Pieced and appliquéd cotton quilted coverlet, probably NJ	Christie's NY	$2,860
1990	Strip quilt of pink-and-white sateen	Christie's U.K.	£242
1990	Pieced cotton quilted coverlet, American, late 19th century	Christie's NY	$1,210
1990	Strip quilt	Christie's U.K.	£38.50
1990	Strip quilt of pale blue and pink sateen	Christie's U.K.	£71.50
1990	Durham quilt of peach-colored sateen, 90" x 74"	Christie's U.K.	£110
1990	Unfinished patchwork coverlet, 80" x 44"	Christie's U.K.	£176
1990	Embroidered and beaded silk-and-velvet crazy crib quilt, American, 1891	Christie's NY	$880
1991	Amish pieced cotton quilted coverlet, probably Midwestern, ca. 1930	Christie's NY	$77
1991	Patchwork quilt, New Castle, Henry County, IN, ca. 1880	Skinner, Inc.	$1,045
1991	Pieced cotton quilted coverlet, American, 19th century	Christie's NY	$2,200
1991	Amish pieced wool quilted coverlet, Lancaster County, PA, ca. 1920	Christie's NY	$2,750
1995	Pieced calico Split Bar quilt	Sotheby's NY	$805
1998	Turkey Red and white strip quilt, 80" x 82"	Christie's U.K.	£207
1998	Turkey Red and white strip quilt, 86" x 96"	Christie's U.K.	£609
1998	Strip quilt	Christie's U.K.	£69
1998	Strip quilt of pale yellow and lemon yellow cotton sateen, 78" x 84"	Christie's U.K.	£207
1998	Strip quilt of sugar pink and white cotton, 86" x 80"	Christie's U.K.	£195
1998	Strip quilt of Turkey Red and white cotton, 70" x 78"	Christie's U.K.	£207
1999	Pieced and appliquéd cotton quilted coverlet	Christie's NY	$173
1999	Strip quilt	Christie's U.K.	£230
2002	A good chintz strip quilt of 1830s and '40s printed cotton	Sotheby's U.K.	£743.20

Sunburst

Year	Description	House	Price
2004	Nine pieced sunbursts in blue, yellow, green, and brown calicos, 19th century, 91" x 87"	Skinner, Inc.	$558.13
2004	Twenty-five blocks centered with a sunburst in red, green, and yellow calico print, mid–19th century, 88" x 89"	Skinner, Inc.	$1,116.25

Tree of Life

Year	Description	House	Price
1987	American pieced cotton Tree of Life pattern quilt, third quarter 19th century	Butterfields	$467.50
1991	Appliquéd quilt, South County, RI, early 19th century	Skinner Inc.	$1,540
1991	Pieced and appliquéd cotton quilted coverlet, Mary Headrick, probably VT, 1810	Christie's NY	$8,250
1992	Pieced and appliquéd cotton quilted coverlet, American, ca. 1830	Christie's NY	$9,900

Skinner sold this Sunburst quilt for $1,116.25 at the fall American furniture and decorative arts auction in 2004. (Photograph courtesy of Skinner, Inc. Bolton, MA)

1998	Pieced cotton Tree of Life quilt, 80" x 81"	Butterfields	$690
1998	Pieced cotton Tree of Life quilt, mid–19th century	Butterfields	$862.50
1998	Pieced cotton Tree of Life quilt, 80" x 80"	Butterfields	$920
1999	Unusual pieced cotton Amish quilt, OH, ca. 1930	Sotheby's NY	$1,150
2005	Quilt of 16 blocks separated with green patterned border, 75" x 75"	Winter Associates	$252
2005	Made by Esther Yoder, ca. 1945, 76" x 95"	Pook & Pook, Inc.	$259

Tulip

Year	Description	House	Price
2002	Cotton quilt of red and apple green on white ground, rom Nina Wilson Creel, who lived in the "Seven Mile House," Davisville, WV, 69" x 81"	Ken Farmer Auctions & Appraisals, LLC	$230

A Tulip pattern quilt that sold in 2003 for $2,115. (Photograph courtesy of Skinner, Inc. Bolton, MA)

2003	Composed of nine red cotton and green printed calico tulip and flower blossoms, 19th century, 84" x 86"	Skinner, Inc.	$2115
2003	Greens, browns, and red, 79" x 59½"	Ken Farmer Auctions & Appraisals, LLC	$250
2003	Roses and tulips with foliage in geometric panels, enclosed in urn and tulip border, 6' 3" x 6' 5"	Ken Farmer Auctions & Appraisals, LLC	$800
2004	Blue-and-orange potted tulip quilt, late 19th century, approximately 88" x 88"	Sotheby's NY	$1,800
2004	Bright pink-and-green tulips appliquéd on a white ground, figure-eight quilting in the border, 80" x 92"	Alderfer Auction Company	$195.50
2004	Trapunto, late 19th century, 81½" x 83"	Ken Farmer Auctions & Appraisals, LLC	$400
2004	Orange/yellow latticework surrounding red-and-green tulip sprays, figure-eight quilting on border, 89" x 92"	Alderfer Auction Company	$805
2004	PA, 19th century	Pook & Pook, Inc.	$750
2004	Tulip decoration in pinks and greens rising out of blue triangles, 74" square	Alderfer Auction Company	$287.50
2004	Red, green, and yellow on a cream field, late 19th/early 20th century, 92" x 72½"	Ken Farmer Auctions & Appraisals, LLC	$330
2005	Early 20th century, 74" x 86"	Pook & Pook, Inc.	$633
2005	MO, ca. 1870, 86" x 88"	Pook & Pook, Inc.	$920
2005	PA, ca. 1870, 88" x 102"	Pook & Pook, Inc.	$460
2005	Red-and-green tulips surrounded by serpentine floral border with birds, 80" x 80"	Ken Farmer Auctions & Appraisals, LLC	$522.50

Tumbling Blocks

Year	Description	House	Price
1987	American pieced calico Tumbling Blocks pattern quilt, late 19th century	Butterfields	$1,430
1988	Victorian Tumbling Blocks quilt panel, late 19th century	Butterfields	$522.50
1990	Patchwork quilt, American, late 19th/early 20th century	Skinner, Inc.	$880
1991	Wool-and-cotton quilted coverlet, American, 19th century	Christie's NY	$6,050
1992	Pieced wool-and-cotton quilted coverlet, American, ca. 1880	Christie's NY	$1,100
1992	Amish quilt in Tumbling Block pattern, initialed "E. L. S.," dated 1963, 76" x 86½"	James Julia	$500
1992	Pieced and appliquéd wool-and-cotton quilted coverlet, American, ca. 1930s	Christie's NY	$88
1998	Appliquéd cotton Tumbling Blocks variant quilt, 72" x 76"	Butterfields	$920
1998	Pieced cotton Tumbling Blocks variant quilt, 79" x 90"	Butterfields	$747.50
1998	Pieced cotton Tumbling Block quilt, 78" x 82"	Butterfields	$2,587.50
2001	Amish cotton T Blocks and Bars quilt, ca. 1920	Butterfields	$1,116.25

2003	Victorian, 65" x 68"	Winter Associates	$280
2004	Victorian, bright colors, 82" x 82"	Winter Associates	$308
2005	PA, late 19th century, 85" x 100"	Pook & Pook, Inc.	$431

Wandering Foot

Year	Description	House	Price
1998	Pieced and appliquéd cotton Wandering Foot quilt	Butterfields	$1,150

Whig Rose

Year	Description	House	Price
1990	Pieced and appliquéd cotton quilted coverlet, American, late 19th/early 20th century	Christie's NY	$1,540
1990	Pieced and appliquéd cotton quilted coverlet, probably NJ	Christie's NY	$2,860
1992	Pieced and appliquéd cotton quilted coverlet, American, early 20th century	Christie's NY	$165
1992	Pieced and appliquéd cotton quilted coverlet, American, second half 19th century	Christie's NY	$385
1996	American pieced and appliqué cotton quilt	Sloan's DC	$750

Whitework

Year	Description	House	Price
1998	Fine all-white cotton bride's quilt, signed "Abby Caroline Smith, East Lyme, Connecticut, March 1840"	Sotheby's NY	$3,162
1999	Coverlet of ivory cotton	Christie's U.K.	£103
1999	Whitework quilted cotton coverlet	Christie's NY	$1,840

Whole Cloth

Year	Description	House	Price
1998	Double-sided whole-cloth joined quilt of white cotton sateen, 84" x 68"	Christie's U.K.	£207
1998	Joined whole-cloth quilt, 76" x 80"	Christie's U.K.	£299
1998	Joined whole-cloth quilt, 96" x 84"	Christie's U.K.	£207
1998	Joined whole-cloth quilt of cotton sateen, 80" x 82"	Christie's U.K.	£276
1998	Joined whole-cloth quilt of sage green cotton sateen, 80" x 88"	Christie's U.K.	£69
1999	Joined whole-cloth quilt, 80" x 80"	Christie's U.K.	£195
1999	Joined whole-cloth quilt, 80" x 90"	Christie's U.K.	£345
1999	Joined whole-cloth quilt, 80" x 96"	Christie's U.K.	£92
1999	Joined whole-cloth quilt, 84" x 80"	Christie's U.K.	£126
1999	Joined whole-cloth quilt, 86" x 84"	Christie's U.K.	£34
1999	Joined whole-cloth quilt of ivory cotton sateen	Christie's U.K.	£34

| 2004 | Dark Green, quilted in a Diamond pattern centered with a pinwheel, 111" x 102" | Skinner, Inc. | $1,057.50 |
| 2005 | Floral pattern, mid–19th century, 104" x 108" | Pook & Pook, Inc. | $240 |

Yo-Yo

Year	Description	House	Price
2001	Large, colorful Yo-Yo quilt, 86" x 50"	James Julia	$57.50

Inscribed "William Ann Norville 1823-1911 Temperance Hall North Carolina," this Starburst quilt sold for $4,950 at a 2004 Thomaston Place Auction Galleries sale. (Photograph courtesy of Thomaston Place Auction Galleries)

Part 2

Quilt Patterns from Famous Estate Sales

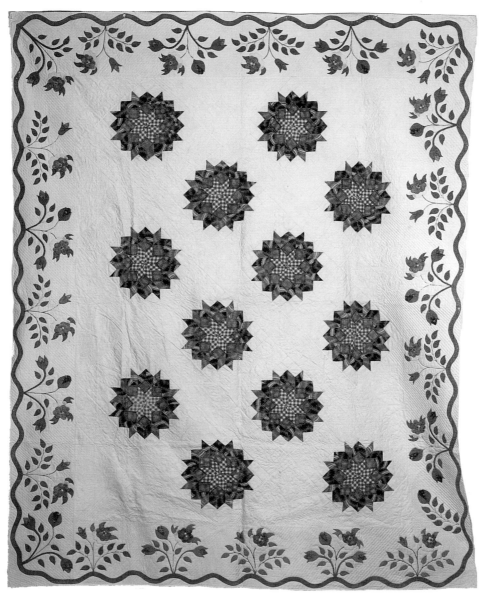

This 1870-1880 Star quilt was estimated at $300-$500. It was sold in 2004 by Cowan's Auctions for $1,265. (Photograph courtesy of Cowan's Auctions, Inc.)

This quilt, circa 1840-1860, bearing the inscription "William Ann Norville 1823-1911 Temperance Hall North Carolina" was sold for $3,850 in 2004. (Photograph courtesy of Thomaston Place Auction Galleries)

6

Making Your Own Quilt Reproduction

One aspect of antique quilts that serves as a continual source of inspiration for modern quilters is the precision and detail found in the stitching or quilting. Applied in intricate patterns with a typically impressive stitches-per-inch density, the stitching of vintage quilts is a remarkable demonstration of outstanding craftsmanship. For the quilter attempting to create a reproduction of an antique quilt, duplicating vintage quilting patterns can be an arduous task. No place is this challenge greater than in creating a reproduction of a quilt that you coveted at a recent auction house sale.

Attending an auction or estate sale will sharpen your eye for learning to discriminate between good quilting and outstanding quilting. A discriminating eye is as vital a tool for the traditional quilter as a trustworthy ruler. In the realm of antique quilt collecting, a discriminating eye can mean the difference between finding a work of art and being fooled by a cast-off remnant.

The results of one such trained eyed were auctioned off by Sotheby's on June 16, 1998. Gathered into the property from the Sotheby's auction of the late Richard C. von Hess's estate were three antique quilt gems. The fact that Sotheby's auctions occasionally feature outstanding quilts should come as no surprise; because these quilts were from the Richard C. von Hess estate, however, does indicate that all three quilts were of considerable merit. To fully appreciate the impact of this lofty statement, you must first learn about the quilts' collector.

Richard von Hess was an extraordinary collector of exquisite American art and artifacts. In fact, von Hess was known by art dealers in England as "the American with the best eye." Be assured therefore that the quilts occupying a small niche in the von Hess estate were superlative representatives of early American quilting.

Leading this triumvirate of nineteenth-century quilting was an American Pillar pattern measuring $92\frac{1}{2}$ inches by $91\frac{1}{4}$ inches featuring bands of cotton chintz alternating with Postage Stamp diamonds pieced into pillars. The backside was quilted with interlocking circles. The color selection was a warm earthtone combination of tan, brown, green, red, and ocher. Sotheby's had estimated that this quilt would fetch a winning bid of $600 to $800. In reality, the winning bid was $1,495.

The second most remarkable quilt in the von Hess estate was an Amish pieced Bar quilt estimated by Sotheby's at $2,000 to $3,000. Designed around a central square formed from nine alternating bars of grape- and dark-brown-colored cotton, this treasure ably demonstrated the Amish mastery of precise quilting. Stitched pineapples and feathers filled a dark red border that outlined the central square. An ample gray border with purple squares in each corner was quilted with a perfectly balanced outline of Fruit Basket quilting. This Amish pieced Bar quilt measuring $77\frac{1}{4}$ inches by 74 inches was sold for a bid of $3,737.

Closing out the von Hess estate were two pieced Star of Bethlehem quilts, which formed an unbelievable visual treat when held in close juxtaposition. The larger of the two quilts sported a brightly colored central star medallion on a red ground with a teal-and-pink serrated border centered on a wide teal border quilted with interlacing bands. Conversely, the second and smaller quilt incorporated duller tones on a cream ground with pieced stars situated between each ray of the central star. In pre-auction catalogs, Sotheby's had estimated that this $79\frac{1}{2}$-inch by 82-inch Star of Bethlehem quilt duo would bring a bid of $1,000 to $1,500. Displaying their keen eye for accuracy in bid predictions, the winning bid was $1,380.

A workhorse that can master every quilting challenge—the Janome Memory Craft 10000.

Hand Quilting

In each case, the von Hess quilts were undoubtedly hand-quilted quilts. If you are an experienced quilter, you probably have a preferred method for performing hand quilting. The two generally accepted methods for hand quilting are:

Hoop. This a traditional method for hand quilting that is valued for its portability. In order to hand quilt with a hoop, the quilt's layers must be securely basted together. Next the hoop should be placed in the center of the quilt and moved towards the outside edges as the quilting evolves.

Frame. Although cumbersome in its structure, a quilting frame eliminates the need for basting the quilt's layers together. Held onto the frame with muslin strips, the quilt is moved across the frame using a ratchet gear system. The quilting is performed on the taut quilt as it is firmly held by the gear system. When the quilting has been completed for an area, the ratchet is wound and the quilt is advanced to a new area.

Hand Quilting

Equipment	Hoop or Frame
Thread	Quilting Thread
Needle	8 or 9
Stitches per Inch	9-12
Time*	400 hours

* According to Stearns Technical Textiles Company

Before you buy all of your fabric, create a sample quilt block. After you have completed this sample, you'd better love the results. There is a lot of effort that goes into a quality quilt and you don't want to tire of your quilt before it is completed.

Machine Quilting

Equipment	Sewing machine w/quilt stitch
Thread	.004 Nylon & Cotton Thread
Needle	65/9 or 70/10
Stitches per Inch	6
Time*	40 hours

* According to Stearns Technical Textiles Company

Machine Quilting

Another method of quilting that is quickly becoming more accepted by quilters is machine quilting. Tracing its roots to the 1870s, machine quilting has witnessed a recent boom due to the development of professional sewing machines capable of delivering accurate quilt-stitch reproductions.

While you could argue that the invention of the sewing machine was a collaborative effort derived from the individual contributions of several inventors, one thing is certain, the sewing machine was not invented by Isaac Merit Singer. Long

considered a truism in American inventor's lore, Singer's most noteworthy contributions to the development of the sewing machine were a knack for marketing, a piston needle-movement mechanism, a treadle power supply, and most importantly losing a patent infringement lawsuit filed by Elias Howe.

Howe was the struggling father of the sewing machine who labored his entire life teetering near bankruptcy only to see patent infringements like Singer's steal his discovery. In bitter irony, Howe's patent lawsuit was upheld in 1854 and in 1856 he was awarded a royalty for every sewing machine sold in America, thus making the destitute Howe a millionaire; but, his wealth was short-lived. The frail inventor died in 1867 at the age of forty-eight.

Recently, a trend has rocked today's sewing machine market that is as revolutionary today as the original sewing machine was in 1845.[1] Many of the leading sewing machine manufacturers, like Janome America, Inc. (formerly The New Home Sewing Machine Company), have begun incorporating computer systems inside the sewing machine's chassis, including large, full-color touch screen displays that control everything from stitch selection to the convenient display of basic sewing and embroidery help information.

Consider using lingerie thread when fine thread is needed for projects such as appliqué quilts.

Unveiled at a lavish Caesars Palace, Las Vegas, ceremony in 2000, the Janome Memory Craft 10000 became the first sewing machine to seamlessly integrate an external computer into the sewer's and quilter's workspace. Furthermore, by including three powerful, easy-to-use computer interfaces into its sewing machine, an ATA PC (Advanced Technology Attachment-Personal Computer) card slot, a serial port, and, most importantly, a sleek and fast USB (Universal Serial Bus) port, Janome has enabled the Memory Craft 10000 to be conveniently upgraded with new software. In fact, Memory Craft 10000 owners can download these software upgrades directly from the Janome Web site (www.janome.com) for immediate installation into the sewing machine via any of its three built-in interfaces. The result is a powerful sewing/quilting workstation that can be upgraded with feature enhancements throughout the life of the machine.

While the Memory Craft 10000 is primarily intended for integration with Intel-based computer systems, Apple® Power

Macintosh owners aren't left out in the cold. By using an affordable PC-emulation program (e.g., Connectix Virtual PC; www.connectix.com), virtually any modern USB-equipped Mac easily can be interfaced with the Memory Craft 10000.

Now what does all of this elaborate computerization provide the quilter? There are four programming areas in which the Memory Craft 10000 stands head and shoulders above the competition. First, an authentic French Knot is programmed into the machine as an heirloom decorative stitch. Additionally, there is a great Rolled Hem stitch package (complete with presser foot) that is ideal for making appliqué floral stems. Finally, there are three pre-programmed quilting techniques: appliqué, patchwork, and quilting. When you access one of these techniques, you are visually guided by the full-color touch screen display for selecting the proper presser foot (both a wonderful $\frac{1}{4}$" Seam Foot and a Walking Foot are included with the Memory Craft 10000) and setting the stitch width, length, and thread tension, as well as enabling the quilter to chose between various stitches (e.g., blanket, appliqué, zigzag, new sculpture, clasp, and free quilting). Couple these stitch packages with its built-in, professional-style embroidery capabilities and the Janome Memory Craft 10000 is the ideal quilter's companion.

> To prevent your thread from unraveling when hand quilting, pull the thread off the spool, cut the thread, and knot the end. Now thread the opposite end into the needle.

Variegated color thread patterns, such as those manufactured by Superior Threads, are becoming popular with modern machine quilters.

While YLI Corporation offers line of fine silk and cotton threads that are perfect for professional hand stitching and quilting. On the other hand, the YLI Select line of 100 percent cotton thread is great for piecing, appliqué, and background quilting with a machine.

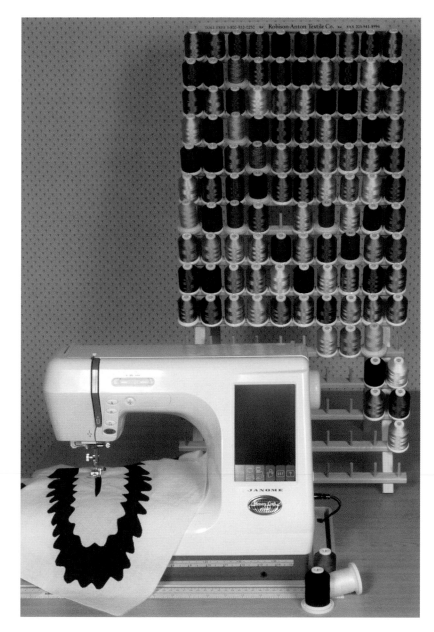

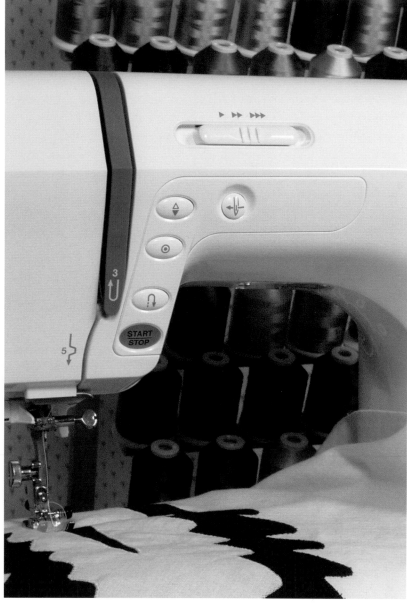

Robison-Anton 1,100 yard spools can be conveniently stored on a special wooden display kit.

The MC 10000 can be easily rethreaded for making fast color changes, and a wide variety of presser feet helps in mastering every quilting challenge.

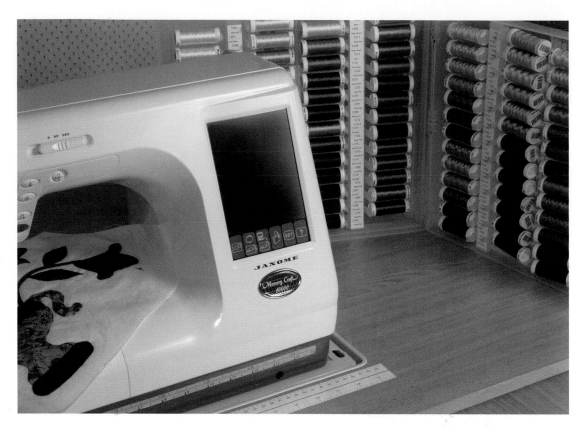

Sulky Slimline Thread Storage Boxes come in three quilter selections: Quilter's Starter Package, Quilter's Dream Package 1, and Quilter's Dream Package 2. These #30 weight rayon thread selections are a high-quality thread that can be used for either hand or machine quilting.

The 500 yard #50 weight 100 percent cotton Robison-Anton thread can be used for either machine or hand appliqué.

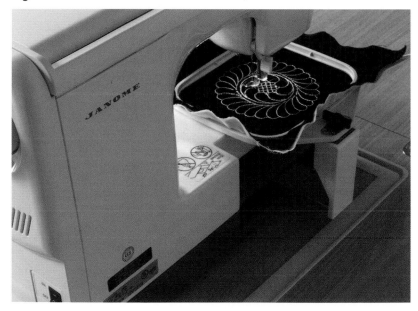

A built-in embroidery system makes quilting elaborate patterns fast and easy.

Even the most complex quilting pattern can be precisely controlled on the color screen of the MC 10000.

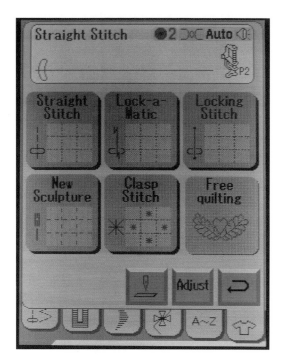

There are six stitching options built into the MC 10000: straight, lock-a-matic, locking, new sculpture, clasp, and free quilting.

There are three sewing patterns that are built into the Janome Memory Craft 10000 (MC 1000): appliqué, blanket stitch, and zigzag stitch.

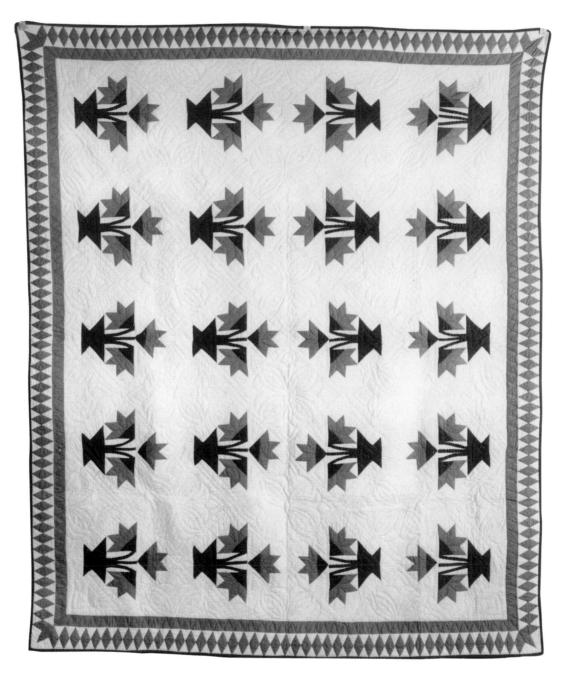

This Carolina Lily pattern quilt was sold for $550 in 1999. (Photograph courtesy of Sloan's)

7

Making Your Own Patterns

If you have ever attended an auction and failed to realize a winning bid for a highly sought-after quilt, welcome to the party. Don't be too heartbroken, though. Instead, you can create your own reproduction of this lost antique quilt. Reproductions also work well when you want to preserve your recently acquired heirloom quilt but would also like a quilt for everyday display purposes.

For example, there was an antique quilt with which we fell in love during a Sotheby's auction. It was a quilt attributed to an African American woman and we just had to have it. At the time, one of the fastest-growing segments of antique collecting was black memorabilia. Whether the artifacts depicted the oppression of slavery, the inequality of discrimination, or the abuse of civil rights, their sales were booming in America's auction houses. Recently, this sales activity has extended into the fiber arts, and quilts made by black women are finally appearing in the marketplace.

Although today's popularity makes the collecting of black memorabilia an obvious selection, forty years ago the notion of owning African American antiques was deemed a risky venture that was far removed from traditional Americana collections. Then along came collector and curator Herbert Waide Hemphill, Jr. Affectionately known as "Bert," Mr. Hemphill was the driving force behind the establishment of today's grassroots American folk art. In fact, Bert's legacy is so secure that he is referred to as the founder of American folk-art collecting. Bert had an uncanny ability for spotting the unique antique amid piles of the commonplace. It was this ability for separating gems from chaff that coined the phrase a "Hemphill thing." Americana artifacts that were outcast by mainstream collectors became cherished treasures to Bert. And in Bert's vocabulary African American antiques were "Hemphill things."

On January 16 and 17, 1999, Sotheby's organized an auction of important American furniture and folk art in honor of the memory of Mr. Hemphill's significant collecting efforts. Inside this sale of over six hundred items was a beautiful 76-inch by 64-inch quilt attributed to a Southern black woman. This quilt has been dated circa late nineteenth or early twentieth century. In his provenance, Robert Bishop also believed that this quilt is from Georgia. While much of its historical origins are vague, it is in this quilt's assembly techniques where the real worth is hidden.

Consisting of thirty red turtles pieced onto a pale yellow field in the Robbing Peter to Pay Paul pattern, this quilt showcases many of the contemporary techniques seen in modern pieced quilting. In this case, each of the turtle's heads and tails are stuffed with a wad of natural cotton. Some of these cotton balls, in fact, still retain some plant debris from poor or hasty cleaning.

In another acknowledgment to modern pieced quilting, this Turtle Quilt also sported white shirt buttons as eyes for each of the thirty red turtles. This effect provided the quilt with an exotic three-dimensional appearance. Rounding out the physical design of this quilt, a white binding had been applied as a frame around the pale yellow field.

Along with its interesting piecework, this quilt also has been publicly displayed a substantial number of times. An exhibition at Hirschl & Adler Folk Art, New York in 1991 featured this quilt. Likewise, one book (*Twentieth Century Quilts 1900-1950,* by Thomas K. Woodard and Blanche Greenstein) from the late 1980s provides literature citations for this Turtle Quilt. It is this rich public record that helped drive the estimated sale price to $12,000 to $15,000. The final sale price realized for this Turtle Quilt was $12,650, making this antique truly a Hemphill thing—but, unfortunately, this quilt did not become our thing.

Note the wonderful elements in this quilt: the Robbing Peter to Pay Paul pattern variation, the stuffed cotton-ball tails and heads, and the white shirt-button turtle eyes. At a Sotheby's auction in 1999, the original quilt was auctioned for $12,650.

Reproducing Lost Bids

Since we were unsuccessful in bidding for this landmark quilt, we decided to create a reproduction of it. Please do not misinterpret "reproduction" as a "fake" or a "forgery." As discussed throughout this book, a reproduction quilt is just that: a representation of a historic quilt and *not* a replacement. By combining today's historic reproduction fabric collections with pattern matching, you can create your own quilt reproduction of an heirloom quilt. Be forewarned, however, as making a quilt reproduction is time consuming. For example, the following quilt reproduction for the Turtle Quilt pattern took us over six months to complete—truly a labor of love and an homage to the original quilt's maker.

We began our reproduction with our trusty Apple® Power Macintosh computer, which was used for rendering the Turtle Quilt pattern. Although there are numerous computer-aided design (CAD) programs on the market for creating patterns, we have found that Adobe Illustrator is ideal for generating quilt patterns. Adobe Illustrator is a vector-based application that draws lines by using coordinate definitions rather than placing individual pixels or dots. This use of vectors versus pixels produces smoother lines and more graceful curves, the essential elements needed for creating appliqué quilt patterns.

The first step in attempting to reproduce this Turtle Quilt was to create a template for tracing the various pattern pieces. To achieve this step, we simply scanned the quilt's photograph in the sale catalog into our Power Mac and placed this image as a template in Adobe Illustrator. During the scanning process, make sure that the final image's dimensions match the proportions of the actual quilt. You can usually find the quilt's dimensions in the lot's description in the catalog. Next, we drew the rough outline of the appliqué's various pieces. Finally, we fine-tuned each appliqué to an exact reproduction of the original.

Prior to the actual piecing and quilting, the final step in making the pattern of the Turtle Quilt was generating a print of the pattern. It is during this step that another strong virtue of Adobe Illustrator comes into play. The output from Adobe Illustrator is defined in a special language known as PostScript. PostScript is a set of instructions that most printers use for making accurate reproductions of artwork and graphic design layouts. By using Adobe Illustrator, PostScript, and a special PostScript laser printer, we were able to make a set of full-size appliqué patterns for the Turtle Quilt. Following an enjoyable several months of quilting, we had created our own reproduction of a quilt that we had previously lost on the auction block.

Complex designs like this crazy quilt are extremely difficult to reproduce, but this pattern is ideal for being customized with your own personalized quilting technique.

Templates and tools from Wright EZ Quilting make the drafting of quilting patterns like Drunkard's Path a snap.

The original "Scenes of Childhood" quilt was sold by Skinner in 2002 for $30,550. (Photograph courtesy of Skinner, Inc. Boston, MA)

8

A Sampler of Four Antique Quilts

During the course of nine years (1994-2003), the major auction houses experienced an explosion in the sale of antique quilts. Quilt lots were regularly featured in almost every major sale of Americana auctioned by Butterfields, Skinner, Sotheby's, and Christie's. In 1999, houses like Sloan's and James D. Julia also began to offer quilts in their American folk-art sales. This proliferation of quilt sales has provided quilt historians with the unique opportunity to examine some of the most significant quilts ever made.

"Scenes of Childhood" Quilt

One of the most famous quilts ever sold at an auction might be this late-nineteenth-century quilt titled "Scenes of Childhood." Featured in the Los Angeles County Museum of Art's "Wrapped in Glory: Figurative Quilts and Bedcovers 1700-1900" exhibition in 1990-1991 (in fact, this quilt was the "poster" child for the exhibition: it was used for the show's poster), as well as in Sandi Fox's book *Small Endearments: Nineteenth-Century Quilts for Children and Dolls* (Rutledge Hill Press, Nashville, TN, 1985, 1994), this diminutive 37 x 35-inch quilt was innocently and simply listed by Skinner, Inc. during its November 2, 2002, auction in Boston as an "embroidered and appliquéd cotton quilt." Estimated to bring a price between $25,000 and $35,000, the "Scenes of Childhood" quilt was sold at auction for $30,550.

An oddity that figures very prominently in the design of this landmark quilt is the use of drawings, facial-feature embellishments, and captions penned with India ink that are successfully intermingled with the more traditional forms of quilting. In fact, there are three captions associated with the main figurative blocks of this quilt: "Here's some more sins in my pottet," "Gran-pa ride first," and "Dolly is sick." While the second and third captions are rather self-explanatory, the first caption

demands some interpretation. Anne Trodella, the director of public relations with Skinner, Inc., was able to supply this plausible explanation: "I spoke with the woman who catalogued the quilt. She said the quote is correct as entered in the catalog. It apparently was written as the child spoke [in baby talk] the word 'sins' [things] and 'pottet' [pocket]." This kind of help provided by Anne is an excellent example of the type of assistance that you can always get from a reputable auction house.

NOTE: In Sandi Fox's aforementioned book, *Small Endearments,* the first two captions are erroneously described as "Here's some more sins in my pocket" and "Grandpa ride first."

"Dolly is sick." Layered appliqué is used in this reproduction.

A close approximation of the quilting pattern from the "Scenes of Childhood" quilt.

A fabric palette is the first step in making this "Scenes of Childhood" quilt reproduction. We used YLI Corporation 100 percent long-staple cotton Select thread for all appliqué, piecing, and quilting and Sulky rayon embroidery thread for adding all stitching details and embellishments.

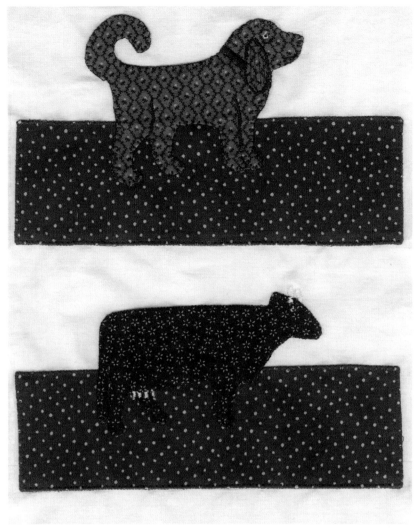

Cornucopia blocks from the corners of this "Scenes of Childhood" quilt reproduction.

The dog and cow appliqué from the quilt reproduction.

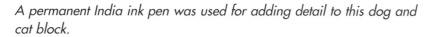

"Here's some more sins in my pottet." This reproduction includes permanent-ink facial details.

A permanent India ink pen was used for adding detail to this dog and cat block.

Gran. Pa ride first

"Gran-pa ride first" is embroidered with Sulky rayon thread on this reproduction.

Patriotic Union Quilt

This is the tale of two quilts—actually, only one quilt, but it was sold by two different auction houses three years apart! This quilt's first appearance at an auction sale was at Sotheby's in New York on January 16, 1999. Listed as a "Union" quilt, probably from Pennsylvania, circa 1915, this quilt sold for $8,050 at this auction. Just three years later, at Skinner, Inc. in Boston on November 2, 2002, the same quilt, now described as a "pieced and appliquéd cotton Union quilt, probably Pennsylvania, c. 1915," sold for $9,988. That is roughly a 24 percent return on a three-year investment. Oddly enough, however, the dimensions of the quilt when it was sold at Sotheby's were listed as 76 x 76 inches, while Skinner sized the quilt at 68 x 75 inches.

All the quilting and piecing for our reproduction was performed on a Janome MC 10000 with Robison-Anton #50 weight 100 percent cotton thread.

A drawing of an eagle from the Union quilt.

The original Union quilt, circa 1915, sold by Skinner in 2002 for $9,988.
(Photograph courtesy of Skinner, Inc. Boston, MA).

Amish-Tribute-to-Charles Lindbergh Quilt

One of the earliest major auction house sales of quilts was the September 1996 estate auction by Sloan's in Washington, D.C., which featured twenty-five unique quilts. Hidden among the more popular Star, crazy, and Log Cabin patterns was an unusual Amish quilt commemorating the 1927 Atlantic Ocean flight of Charles Lindbergh and his aircraft, *The Spirit of St. Louis.*

Attributed to the Ohio Amish and dated as March 1933, this quilt featured a sumptuous combination of rose, yellow, green, purple, gray, blue, and black cotton fabrics arranged in a variation of the Rail Fence pattern, which was interpreted by Sloan's as a "propeller" pattern. In a nod to Lindbergh's accomplishment, the quilt maker had stitched an inscription reading "Spirit of Saint Louis" in the quilt's purple border. Estimated at between $1,600 and $1,800, this quilt realized a winning bid of $1,100 at auction.

Mountain Mist polyester batting was used for maintaining a thin, low-loft appearance in a finished quilt.

A Spirit of Saint Louis *reproduction quilt.*

Mennonite Star Quilt

The early auction house sales of quilts included some excellent examples of well-documented historical patterns. One such quilt from a Sotheby's auction on October 23, 1994, was a Mennonite Star from Pennsylvania made during the latter half of the nineteenth century. The provenance for this quilt was attributed to Robert E. Kinnaman and Brian A. Ramaekers of Houston, Texas. Based on this wealth of supporting data, Sotheby's had placed an estimated value of $2,000 to $4,000 on this quilt. At auction the winning bid was $2,300.

Poly-fil natural cotton batting helped stabilize this Mennonite Star quilt for receiving its elaborate quilting pattern.

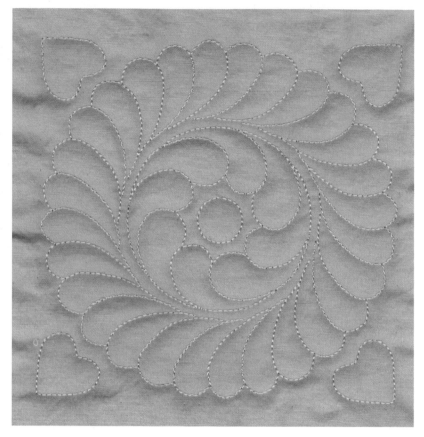

A large embroidery hoop on a Janome Memory Craft 10000 (MC 1000) stitched this quilting pattern in under six minutes!

The original Mennonite Star quilt, which served as the inspiration for this reproduction, was sold for $2,300 at a 1994 auction.

This quilt, which sold for $3,450 at a 2004 Cowan's Auctions sale, was purported to have been entered in the Sears National Quilt Contest at the 1933 Chicago World's Fair. (Photograph courtesy of Cowan's Auctions, Inc.)

Appendixes

A. Auction House Directory

Alderfer Auction Company
501 Fairgrounds Road
Hatfield, PA 19440
www.alderferauction.com

Auctions by the Bay, Inc.
2700 Saratoga Street
Alameda, CA 94501
www.auctionsbythebay.com

Robert S. Brunk Auction Services, Inc.
P.O. Box 2135
Asheville, NC 28802
www.brunkauctions.com

Bonhams & Butterfields
220 San Bruno Avenue
San Francisco, CA 94103
www.butterfields.com or www.bonhams.com

Christie's
20 Rockefeller Plaza
New York, NY 10020
www.christies.com

Cowan's Auctions, Inc.
673 Wilmer Avenue
Cincinnati, OH 45226
(513) 231-5115
www.cowanauctions.com

*This Harvest Sun pattern quilt sold for $2,585 at a 2003 auction.
(Photograph courtesy of Skinner, Inc. Bolton, MA)*

Dargate Auction Galleries
214 N. Lexington Street
Pittsburgh, PA 15208
www.dargate.com

Ken Farmer Auctions & Appraisals, LLC
105 Harrison Street
Radford, VA 24141
www.kfauctions.com

Garth's Auctions, Inc.
2690 Stratford Road
P.O. Box 369
Delaware, OH 43015
www.garths.com

Guernsey's
108 E. 73rd Street
New York, NY 10021
www.guernseys.com

Jackson's International Auctioneers & Appraisers
Lincoln Street
Cedar Falls, IA 50613
(319) 277-2256
www.jacksonsauction.com

James D. Julia
P.O. Box 830
Fairfield, ME 04937
www.juliaauctions.com

New Orleans Auction Galleries, Inc.
801 Magazine Street
New Orleans, LA 70130
www.neworleansauction.com

Northeast Auctions
93 Pleasant Street,
Portsmouth, NH 03801-4504
www.northeastauctions.com

Pook & Pook, Inc. Auctioneers and Appraisers
463 East Lancaster Avenue
Downingtown, PA 19335
(610) 269-0695
www.pookandpook.com

Dan Ripley's Antique Helper Auctions
2764 E. 55th Place
Indianapolis, IN 46220
www.danripley.com

Skinner, Inc.
The Heritage on the Garden
63 Park Plaza
Boston, MA 02116
(978) 779-6241
www.skinnerinc.com

Sloan's Auction Galleries
Washington DC Gallery
4920 Wyaconda Road
N. Bethesda, MD 20852
www.sloansauction.com

Sotheby's
1334 York Avenue
New York, NY 10021
www.sothebys.com

Stair Galleries
P.O. Box 418
Claverack, NY 12513
www.stairgalleries.com

Thomaston Place Auction Galleries
P.O. Box 300
51 Atlantic Highway, US Rt. 1
Thomaston, ME 04861
www.thomastonauction.com

Winter Associates, Inc.
21 Cooke Street
P.O. Box 823
Plainville, CT 06062
www.auctions-appraisers.com

B. Suppliers' Names & Addresses

Batting

Fairfield Processing Corp
P.O. Box 1130
Danbury, CT 06813
(800) 243-0989
www.poly-fil.com

Mountain Mist, The Stearns Technical Textiles Company
100 Williams Street
Cincinnati, OH 45215
(800) 345-7150
www.stearnstextiles.com

The Warm Company
954 East Union Street
Seattle, WA 98122
www.warmcompany.com

Cutting Tools

Fiskars Inc.
305 84th Avenue South
Wausau, WI 54401
www.fiskars.com

Gingher, Inc.
P.O. Box 8865
Greensboro, NC 27419
www.gingher.com

Notions

Wrights, EZ Quilting
West Warren, MA 01092
www.ezquilt.com

Preservation

Archivart
7 Caesar Place
Moonachie, NJ 07074
www.archivart.com

Sewing Machines

Janome America, Inc.
10 Industrial Avenue
Mahwah, NJ 07430
www.janome.com

Templates, Stencils and Rulers

Omnigrid Inc.
P.O. Box 663
Burlington, WA 98233

Scissors like this four-inch Designer's Series by Gingher are great for precise cutting and snipping.

Colorful fabrics, like these from Marcus Brothers' Classic Images by Judie Rothermel, can add a splash of color to a reproduction quilt.

Textiles

Benartex, Inc.
1359 Broadway, Suite 1100
New York, NY 10018
(212) 840-3250
www.benartex.com

Marcus Brothers Textiles, Inc.
1460 Broadway
New York, NY 10046
www.marcusbrothers.com

Debbie Mumm, Inc.
1116 E. Westview Court
Spokane, WA 99218
www.debbiemumm.com

Thread

Robison-Anton
Textile Company
P.O. Box 159
Fairview, NJ 07022
www.robison-anton.com

Sulky of America
3113 Broadpoint Drive
Punta Gorda, FL 33983
Fax: (941) 743-4634
www.sulky.com
www.speedstitch.com
www.uncommonthread.com

Superior Threads
P.O. Box 1672
St. George, UT 84771
www.superiorthreads.com

YLI Corporation
161 West Main Street
Rock Hill, SC 29730
www.ylicorp.com

Updates/Information for This Book

PCo2Go
www.pco2go.com

Fabric manufacturers like Debbie Mumm® offer great collections of historic fabric patterns. Likewise, Warm & Natural is a great batting for reproduction quilts.

This beautiful Star quilt, circa 1870, was sold by Skinner for $1,762.50 at a 2004 summer decorative arts auction. (Photograph courtesy of Skinner, Inc. Bolton, MA)

Notes

Chapter 1

1. Barabara Brackman, "A Chronological Index to Pieced Quilt Patterns: 1775-1825," *Uncoverings* 4 (1983): 99-127.

2. Ibid., 104.

3. Ibid.

4. Stella Rubin, *Miller's Treasure or Not? How to Compare & Value American Quilts* (London, UK: Octopus Publishing Group, Ltd., 2001), 115.

5. Roderick Kiracofe, *The American Quilt: A History of Cloth and Comfort 1750-1950* (New York: Clarkson N. Potter, Inc., 1993), 255.

6. Ibid., 255.

7. James N. Liles, "Dyes in American Quilts Made Prior to 1930, with Special Emphasis on Cotton and Linen," *Uncoverings* 5 (1984): 29-40.

8. Ibid. 33-34.

9. Kiracofe, *The American Quilt,* 92-95.

Chapter 2

1. Ann Poe, ed., *Quilting School: A Complete Guide to Patchwork and Quilting* (Pleasantville, NY: The Reader's Digest Association, Inc., 1993), 168.

2. Phyllis George Brown, "Living with Quilts," *America's Glorious Quilts,* ed. Dennis Duke and Deborah Harding (Hugh Lauter Levin Associates, Inc.), 297.

3. Ibid., 299.

Chapter 6

1. This is the year of the Elias Howe "legendary" demonstration of his sewing machine. During this demonstration, Howe's machine challenged five seamstresses to a sewing contest. While the sewing machine proved successful in winning this competition, Howe was unable to market his sewing machine to the American garment industry.

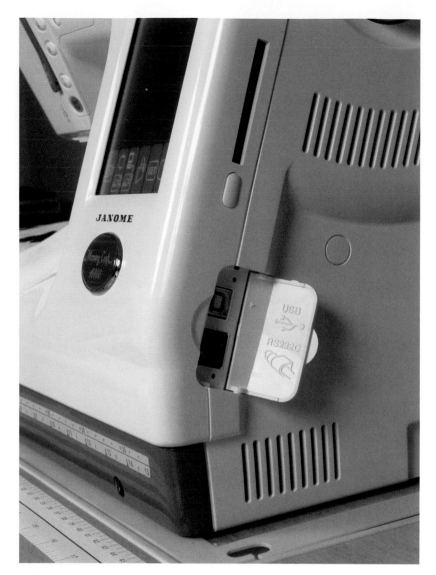

Flexible connection options, like the RS-232C and USB ports and ATA PC slot found on the Janome MC 10000, are invaluable interface features when performing modern machine quilting.

Basket

Carolina Lily Block

Friendship Star Block

Grandmother's Fan Block

Log Cabin Block

Nine Patch Block

Star of the East Block

Pinwheel Block

Star Block

Schoolhouse Block

Figure G-1

Glossary

Appliqué. Fabric pieces are stitched by machine or by hand to the top of a background fabric. Appliqué designs may be any shape or style.

ATA PC. Advanced Technology Attachment—Personal Computer (formerly known as PCMCIA—Personal Computer Memory Card International Association); a PC-card interface for loading embroidery designs into a modern sewing machine.

Basket pattern. See Figure G-1.

Broderie Perse. Typically, a whole-cloth quilt made from appliquéing chintz motifs on a base cloth fabric.

Calico. A cotton fabric with figured patterns.

Carolina Lily pattern. See Figure G-1.

Chintz. A plain-weave cotton fabric with a glazed finish.

Estimate. A price range that the auction house feels could be representative of the quilt's finally selling price. Resist the temptation to use auction house estimates as a guide for dictating your bidding strategy.

French Knot. A tight, decorative knot made from slipping three revolutions of thread around a needle, which is then pierced back down into the background fabric next to the needle's starting point.

Friendship Star pattern. See Figure G-1.

Grandmother's Fan pattern. See Figure G-1.

Log Cabin pattern. See Figure G-1.

Lot. A collection or parcel of articles offered as one item for sale at an auction.

Nine patch pattern. See Figure G-1.

Pinwheel pattern. See Figure G-1.

Provenance. The origin or source of a historical item.

Reserve. A minimum price that has been mutually established by the seller and the auction house.

Robbing Peter to Pay Paul pattern. See Figure G-1.

Sateen. A strong, lustrous long-staple cotton fabric.

Star pattern. See Figure G-1.

Star of the East pattern. See Figure G-1.

USB. Universal Serial Bus; a port for connecting a modern sewing machine to a personal computer.

Index